LIFE IN THE MEADOWLANDS

A Collection of

35 Nature-Themed, Lyric Essays

Don Torino

Life In the Meadowlands

Don Torino leads a bird walk

Harrier Meadow Field Trip

Egrets, a common site, in the NJ Meadowlands

Foreword

Set against the background of the Manhattan skyline, 'Life in the Meadowlands' takes place in a wetlands area of northern New Jersey (NJ) which lies along the Atlantic Flyway, a major migration route for millions of birds. The Meadowlands have been subject to destruction for a few centuries. But in recent years, some small sections of it have been rehabilitated.

The author, Don Torino, President of the Bergen County Audubon Society (BCAS), is an expert in the nature and legislation associated with the NJ Meadowlands. Don leads field trips regularly at parks including Richard Dekorte (Dekorte), Losen Slope Creek, Mill Creek Marsh Trail and Teaneck Creek Conservancy.

The themes in the book such as importance of wetlands and native plants, spiritual connection to nature, and plight of endangered species are universal. Wetlands in coastal Louisiana and the Amazon Basin matter as they do in NJ because they protect against flooding, improve water quality, and provide habitat for many fish and wildlife that are specifically adapted to live there. Similarly, native plants make a difference here in the NJ Meadowlands just as they do in Timbuktu. After co-evolving with plants in particular regions for hundreds of thousands of years, insects and wildlife depend on them for survival and are unable to adjust to influxes of foreign plants in short periods of time. Likewise, endangered species, like the

Taiwanese Leopard Cat, suffer predicaments like many endangered species of birds that concentrate in the Meadowlands due to loss of habitat.

I started spending time in the outdoors after college but lacked knowledge about the natural world. Once when hiking to a glacial lake near Hewitt NJ, a man stopped us to show a leaf. He rubbed it together explaining that it smelled like fruit loops and was called Sassafras (**sa**·suh·fras). It sounded like he went a long way back with this type of leaf, but it was the first time I was hearing about it. I wished I had known about Sassafras longer.

Some years had passed when I started venturing into the Meadowlands. When driving there, about 10 miles before reaching Dekorte, a blue 'entering watershed' sign with an Egret appears on the side of the road. Even though I already know what's there, I sometimes look past the sign expecting to see a beautiful preserve. But buildings and concrete are all that can be seen in every direction for miles. To me, the sign is a reminder that that place of significance has been destroyed.

Luckily, some sections of the meadowlands have been restored. Since having read Don's writings and attended his field trips, nowadays I am better informed about natural surroundings than I was before.

Once at Dekorte, you don't need to go far to be amazed. A bright yellow Goldfinch might pop his head out of the bushes in the parking lot. On a path up a hill, with insects buzzing around, you may spot a Brown Creeper hopping up a tree trunk. Even without binoculars you might see Cedar Waxwings on Crab Apple trees. A few butterflies like Red Admirals or Question Marks may be fluttering around the Purple Coneflowers, one of the best nectar sources on a hot mid-summer day. A little further toward the Lyndhurst Nature Preserve trail, it's easy to spot white Egrets wading in the water. Tree swallows may speed acrobatically through the air around nest boxes. And in another season, you may even see an endangered, Yellow-crowned Night-Heron standing on top of one of the nest boxes where baby Tree Swallows once poked their heads out. There might be Asters on the ground and Yellow Warblers inside the Saltmarsh Cord Grass along the water next to them. Terns are popular at Dekorte. From an inlet, even endangered Least Terns sometimes land on the boardwalk railings. The most amazing spectacle is when Semipalmated Sandpipers, who migrate from Hudson Bay, start flying together. It's beautiful and ephemeral as they change direction together in the Meadowlands sunset.

And at Dekorte you may even come across a unique leaf that looks like a 3 lobed ghost. It's Sassafras! The Spicebush Swallowtail butterfly got its name from the Spicebush because it uses it as a host plant to lay eggs. But the Spicebush Swallowtail uses Sassafras as a host plant as well.

Don also teaches about natural world phenomenon in a meaningful way and once explained, "Migration is always happening. It's Always happening." Although peak migration may happen on specific days in the spring or fall when many birds travel at once, it's also a continual and gradual process happening throughout the entire year.

And more than an educational book, "Life in the Meadowlands" is also poetic. Don writes from the heart as his deep caring about nature intertwines with his whole life. It is difficult to explain what makes certain writing beautiful. It's hard to pinpoint what gives certain pieces that quality that allows readers to visualize the story vividly or to make them pause at certain points to think. But Don's lyrical essays have already captivated many readers in the Bergen County area. Through this book, many more people around the world will have the chance to experience life in the Meadowlands.

Christine Toth

Acknowledgements

Special thanks to Christine Toth for designing and helping to make this book happen.

Contents

Introduction

The New Jersey Meadowlands, Our Meadowlands, is a precious unique wildlife habitat within view of New York City and nestled in the most densely populated state in the country. And yet despite the worst crimes against nature perpetrated upon it, Our Meadowlands has comeback like a phoenix risen from the ashes. Today, we have over 280 bird species documented there, something no one ever thought could ever happen.

I am proud to have grown up and still live in Our Meadowlands. It has given me the lifetime love of nature and has healed my heart and nourished my soul whenever I needed it the most in my life it has been there for me.

The future of this incredible place is still and perhaps will always be at risk. But as long as we walk together along its paths and learn to love it there will always be someone looking out for its future. It is Our New Jersey Meadowlands.

Growing Up Wild

I promised myself when I was young that I would never become one of those old timers that said things like, "Back in my day we walked to school in 6ft of snow uphill with 80 mile an hour winds with no shoes and never complained." Somehow things always seemed better back in the day. But now, with the risk of becoming one of those old timers I have to say as far as kids growing up and nature are concerned, some things were better back in my day.

My family moved to Moonachie, which is deep in the heart of the New Jersey Meadowlands, when I was twelve years old. Even though it was still Bergen County, it was a very different place to grow up. I came from a town where every kid played baseball and football to place where nature was a fundamental part of our childhood. Picking blackberries, hiking the railroad tracks, and making rafts to float on the old clay pits occupied our summer vacations from sunup to sundown, and shockingly enough our parents didn't even think to call the police if we were a little late. Although, at times, I did consider calling the local law enforcement agency myself just for my own protection when my mother would catch me tracking some meadowlands mud into the house.

Our childhood was intertwined and deeply connected to the natural world. The Red-winged blackbirds, Red-tailed Hawks and Great Egrets were an everyday reality to us. We didn't have to wait to switch on Animal Planet to view wildlife, it was just outside the front door.

Over time many factors have allowed our kids to become separated from nature. Urban sprawl has destroyed many local natural places where kids used to play. Overprotection and disconnection from nature by parents has led to making our kids live in fear from everything from a bird to a bee. We need to find new ways to help bring our kids back from the brink of losing their love of nature for good.

Now I haven't completely become that crotchety old man that thinks that everything was better back in the good old days. Some things really do get better like the great nearby nature centers that make it easy for parents to re-introduce our children to nature. Growing up we never could have imagined amazing places like DeKorte Park, Mill Creek Marsh and Teaneck Creek. The environment is much cleaner than when I was growing up and birds like the Osprey, Peregrine Falcon and Bald Eagle have made a dramatic comeback to New Jersey. Great nature centers exist in almost every community or within close driving distance where we can bring our kids and instill in them the real life 3-D movie, nature. In the case of the inner cities, where a natural area is not accessible to kids, we need to find ways to get them there and to also bring more nature education to their classrooms.

Only when people learn to love nature will they fight to protect it. Our kids are the next generation that will battle to keep the water and air clean, protect endangered species and save critical habitat. Fred Rogers (also known as Mister Rogers), our most beloved neighbor once said, "One of the greatest dignities of humankind is that each successive generation is invested in the welfare of each new generation." It is up to us to help our children grow up a like we did, with the love of nature and a little wildness in their hearts.

Song of the Red-Winged Blackbird

Today the "conk-la-ree" call of the Red-Winged Blackbirds filled the marshes. Bald Eagles perched high in the trees watching the ice below begin to break apart. Belted Kingfishers rattled over the river and for a while, for at least as short time, a very special time, all was right in the world again.

It seems that spring may never come, snow piles up like icebergs that line the streets, woolen hats, gloves, and warm boots rule the day. Our staying at home caused by the pandemic and made worse by ice-packed trails and frigid temperatures seem to amplify the thoughts, feelings and fears of things continuing the way they are forever.

But on this day, as I sat on a bench along the river, sun in my face and my feet deep in snow those feelings were to be forgotten and put aside as the Red-winged Blackbird, the "Spirit of the Marsh" presented its marshland melody for the world to hear.

The Red-winged Blackbird has always had a special place in my heart and played an important role throughout my life. From growing up to adulthood, from births to deaths, from sadness to joy, the Red-wing has always been there for me displaying its bright Red epaulets fearless and steady. It has been there when all else seemed to fail and provided me with a consistency and reliability when everything else seemed to be confusing and unclear. And this year again, just when I needed it the most, the Red-wing sang.

On this magnificent morning, as the Red-wings echoed through the reeds, I was assured that Spring would be here soon and that nature like us would be moving ahead in all its glory and with all its many continuing challenges despite our human frailties and doubts.

Our connection to nature has been challenged over the years, out shouted, overshadowed, and covered up by our many distractions. We can decide to overcome this by merely stepping outside and taking in all nature has to give us and at the same time giving a little back as a way to say thank you for it always being there when it is most needed.

Step outside and listen to the Song of the Red-winged Blackbird, it will renew the soul and strengthen the heart. It will remind us that we are still connected to the natural world and stir our spirit and forever bring us back to place where our love of nature will always be part of who we are.

On this magnificent morning I sat back and listened to the Red-wing, and once again I was assured that all would be right in the world.

The Wood Thrush Still Sings

For me, growing up in the Meadowlands, Teterboro Woods was where I first learned about the wonders of the natural world and where I found my lifelong love of the magic of New Jersey Meadowlands.

I will never forget the first Egrets that flew over my head as a young boy. An instant tingling feeling of wilderness entered my soul that has never left me, and yet there is still something in our Meadowlands, something even more magical and mystical that echoes through the woods like an angelic flute. It is the song of the Wood Thrush. Henry David Thoreau once wrote of the Wood Thrush, "Whenever a man hears it, it is a new world and a free country, and the gates of heaven are not shut against him."

Sadly, the song of the Wood Thrush has been heard less and less in the eastern forests. Habitat fragmentation, acid rain, and the loss of habitat here and in Central America contribute to more silent woodlands.

On a warm Sunday morning in June, I hung my binoculars from my neck and with a kind of nervousness walked out of my house to do my breeding bird survey for the NJSEA. There was no need to get in my truck. I only had to walk out my door and cross the street just like when I was a kid, and I was there. Almost like entering a time machine I would be looking for birds in Teterboro Woods, only not like I would have hoped.

Unfortunately, Teterboro Woods has been off limits for many years, and since 9/11 it is totally inaccessible. Yet I was still excited to explore the perimeter of a place that once was like my backyard, full of birds and memories ever engrained into my soul.

As I walked the fence line, I imagined what was on the other side. Did the wild azalea still bloom? Did the clethra light the forest floor like white candelabras and most of all did the Wood Thrush still run the forest floor and did their song still fill the morning air?

I stood still recalling my boyhood adventures which still existed just a few feet on the other side of the fence. I could still see my late brother fixing his glasses and looking up amazed at a Barred Owl, a perfect picture that is with me every day. Then there was the day when we walked together down the trail after our fathers passing, wondering what would happen to our family.

Everything I wanted to bring back was just on the other side of that fence. As much as I tried to reach in and get around it and see the other side, at least in my mind, I could not. If I could just get on the other side everyone would be there just like it used to be. Binoculars, clothes full of mud and the people that I once loved. And then I heard it! Just on the other side of that old fence a song from the past, an ancient song echoing through the trees, "ee-oh-lay, ee-oh-lay." The Wood Thrush was here.

One to the left another to the far right, the echoing song seemed to fill the air from every direction. My heart was instantly filled with relief that after all these years the Wood Thrush were still here. More than 50 years of life, loss, and everything in between the Wood Thrush still had their song. Suddenly everything came back to me with a sense of peace I have not had for many years. The Wood

Thrush was still here in the Meadowlands and, yes, so was I. And for that moment as the Wood Thrush song traveled through the trees, all was as it should be and nothing else in the world mattered.

Nature is always there for us, patiently waiting. Through time and seasons it always calls to us if we could only find the time to listen. Get outside, take in all nature has to offer. It is what our lives are about, intertwined and interwoven with the birds, the flowers, and the people that make up all our lives forever.

A Sweet Tree

A few years back, birders from all over New Jersey and some neighboring states descended upon Losen Slote Creek Park to see if they could get a look at Redpolls and White-winged Crossbills that were generous enough to stop over and give us local folks a thrill. As a multitude of binoculars gazed skyward, I could hear a nice young lady cry out, "There they are on the itchy balls!" I couldn't help but laugh. I hadn't heard the tree referred to by that name for a very, very long time. Of course, the tree that she was so happily denoting was a Liquidambar styraciflua, the Sweetgum Tree.

My first introduction to the Sweetgum goes back to my youth wandering the wild places of Meadowlands with my friend Paul who was a West Virginia transplant. Paul would always give me some of his good old down home backwoods words of wisdom whenever he got a chance, "When your hunting squirrels in the winter always look for the tree with the little balls, they hold plenty of food when all the other trees are empty." As time went on, I never forgot the lessons of my youth and used what I had learned from my West Virginian chum, but this time for a much more gentle purpose, to help me on my birding ventures. Find a Sweetgum in places like DeKorte, Mill Creek and Losen Slote or wherever and you will find birds.

The Sweetgum Tree got its name for the sweet taste and gummy feel of its sap. Early Pioneers and Native Americans used to chew its hard clumps of resin. Its resin could be obtained by stripping off the bark and allowing it to harden. Sweetgums are large trees which grow up to 100 feet tall with straight trunks and up to three feet wide. They grow in woods and along lakes and streams. They are simple to identify by their star-shaped leaves with five pointy lobes and a long stalk. Fully grown leaves are about six inches long, and bright green. In autumn, the leaves turn red. Sweetgum flowers are tiny, greenish, and ball-like that grow in clusters and, of course, there is its spiny ball-like fruit.

If there was ever a perfect wildlife tree it would be the Sweetgum. The nectar produced by the flowers attract pollinators, hummingbirds and thirty-three species of native caterpillars critical to a healthy ecosystem including the Luna Moth, a declining species. And then of course there are those wonderful "little itchy balls", the characteristic woody fruits covered with spikey prickles. Whether you know the name of the tree or not, everyone knows the tree that is guilty of those little brown prickly balls all over the ground in late fall and winter that you find yourself tripping over and the very same ones you loved to throw at friends when you were a kid. These wonderful little wildlife magnets make the inconvenience of the little orbs on the driveway well worth having. The seeds in the gum ball structure look like the Nyjer (thistle) seeds commonly sold for bird food and will attract the same birds as a finch feeder and more. There may be up to 50 seeds in each ball that are loved by birds such as Goldfinches, Crossbills, Redpolls, Chickadees, Red-winged

Blackbirds and even Wild Turkey dine on the little gum ball seeds. The next time you come across one of the seed balls on the ground pick it up and tap the ball in your hand. You will see all the tiny seeds drop out. Those seeds mean survival to many of our winter birds. Recently I read that there are Sweetgum cultivars that produce no seed balls. In my opinion, this should be considered a crime against nature, like having decaffeinated coffee or non-alcoholic beer. Why bother?

For years my neighbor had a beautiful Sweetgum which hung partly over my property. When he cut it down, I lost many of the great bird species that would visit my backyard. Unfortunately, this is what happens to many of the backyard Sweetgums. They are cut down because homeowners get tired of raking up the many balls that get strewn all over their yards. Just in case you are looking for something more environmentally friendly and imaginative with all those Sweetgum balls they can be used in many craft projects that are fun for the whole family. Planting species like the Sweetgum in the Meadowlands and in our backyards is critical to having and keeping a healthy and vibrant ecosystem in our community. It is a plant that plays an important role in providing food for our many bird species here in the Meadowlands and all of New Jersey. This winter when the birds may seem few and far between look for a Sweetgum tree and my bet is you will find the birds.

Lost Birds Forever

I was a twelve-year-old boy, riding my bicycle in a place and time as foreign to me as could ever be imagined. From just a few miles away my family and I entered a different culture, the Meadowlands. My first home was based in concrete and cars and my new one graced with tides, grasses, and birds. I was suddenly thrust into a life that once was dominated by after school baseball and football games to one that was surrounded by adventures in the meadows, walks in the woods, owls, muskrats, roadside produce stands, horse trails and farm animals crossing the road.

As I peddled down this encroaching industrial road, the kind of road that would eventually pave over, dismantle, and forever change much of my beloved childhood Meadowlands, I came to a sudden dead-end. Tired and hot, I stopped near the driveway of a warehouse which I will come to know till this day as a highly invasive species made of steel and concrete. As I took a breath and thought about where my bike ride into the unknown had brought me, I put my foot to the ground and wiped my forehead. Then something happened which is as real and vivid as if it happened this morning. I looked up to see a strange sight as any alien species I have seen in the movies. There in the trees bordering the dead-end street were white birds, with plumes like something I have seen only on TV jungle movies decorating the limbs and making sounds that made a twelve-year-old boy wonder if what he was witnessing was actually happening.

I looked around me wondering why these birds were here and why there was no one else standing by me watching in amazement? What kind of place had my family and I come to live in? Roads, warehouses, and, oh yes, at the same time wildlife struggling against all odds to carry on. I don't recall how long I stayed there gazing up, but I did eventually decide to peddle away. I can remember stopping and looking back at the magical white plumes that will forever become a part of who I am and at the same time would always leave a part of my heart empty forever.

As I came to learn soon after, I had witnessed breeding Snowy Egrets, the very same birds that once were killed by the millions and placed on ladies' hats. But never in my young mind could I ever imagine I would see them so grandly and so close to my home. I can remember telling my newfound friends about my amazing discovery and they kind of shrugging their shoulders and looking at me in much the same way I looked at the Egrets. After all we were just young boys who thought the place where we lived would never and could never change.

Now I am not sure when it was that I returned to see my wonderful birds or how much time lapsed before I peddled my bike once again to bear witness to this natural wonder, but I do know when I got there the birds were gone and my heart just sank. I looked all around in a kind of panic! Maybe I had the wrong street? Could this be real? But as reality finally hit me there were no birds to be seen, no trees, no bird sounds, only concrete and cars. Where had they gone? How could someone do this? Were the birds hurt? Who allowed this to happen? Why was there was no one else standing with me in mourning? The loss compounded with a feeling of extreme loneliness, was no one else wondering what happened or sharing their grief along with me? I became afraid that maybe I was the only one in the entire world who cared. Now only an enormous nothingness stood there, like it never happened or ever existed. My birds were gone forever. I rode back home constantly trying to make some sense of the tragedy I had witnessed. I had no understanding how those images would affect me throughout my life even more than 50 years later.

Now I am not one of those old-timers who think everything was better in the so called good old days. I know our New Jersey Meadowlands is better than it has been in many generations. After all, I grew up witnessing some of the worst crimes against nature that ever could be committed. And now, I have also been blessed to witness the Meadowlands today rising from the ashes into an incredible environmental gem that could ever have been imagined. And, yet it is those losses that stay with me forever.

Through years of environmental successes and even more so through the tough battles, those Snowy egrets in those trees always seem to appear to me. I go back and try to imagine what a 12-year-old boy could have done to stop it. Who should I have told and if I knew then what I know now? But of course, it would not have mattered but that is what loss does to us, it compounds the what ifs and never lets us forget and maybe that's how it has to be.

Today I am blessed to lead people through our Meadowlands, showing everyone the wonders of what could happen when good people who care work together to do what is right. And yes, I do get to show people the great birds like our Snowy Egret that still bless our Meadowlands, but seldom do I talk about my childhood Snowies. Maybe it's too difficult and maybe it's still hard for me to relive, but those Snowy Egrets down that dead end street will always be part of the reason I do what I do. Maybe it's out of respect or reverence or a way to just to heal, but I like to believe the spirit of those very same birds live in the birds that we now get to enjoy.

They say an environmentalist has to believe in a better tomorrow or they could never deal with the losses that seem to always be part of the job. But lets all make each other a promise that no matter who we are, where we live, we will do our best to have no more losses like those Snowy Egrets of my childhood. And promise that we will all stand together and never be the ones standing alone on street watching our birds and our environment disappear for the next generation.

Birding in the Rain

Since I was a young boy one of my most unwavering beliefs in life has been that any time spent outdoors is almost always better than any time spent indoors. Growing up in the Meadowlands from my early schooldays, later to workdays and still today, I have always felt more at home outside than in. As John Muir once said, "Going to the Mountains is going home." Only to me going home always was and is going to the Meadowlands. So, with that unwavering philosophy in mind, it would also stand to reason that birding in the rain is time very well spent.

Now getting to enjoy birding in the rain usually begins with throwing any semblance of common sense to the wind. After all to purposely go out and get wet when every ancient instinct tells you to go to shelter and stay dry does take some practice. But first we should discuss two proven methods of birding in the rain.

The first method is called, "Accidental birding in the rain." This method depends on either the weatherman being totally wrong and the birder ignoring the weather report all together. Now, truth be told, birders have a much more accurate method of forecasting the weather, it's called, "sticking your head out the door and seeing for yourself what it's like outside." Now this system of meteorology though 100% accurate short term can often go awry long-term resulting in, "Birding in the Rain." Add to that the precipitation percentage seems to go way up when you leave the house without a raincoat or boots. Yet for all the times I have squeezed my wallet out like a sponge and removed my wet socks off my feet like peeling a banana, I am still sure I would not have changed anything about those accidental damp days.

After all, if I would have opted for staying inside, I may have never seen a Great Horned Owl wet as could be and never knew how small it looks when the feathers are drenched due to its special silent flying feather not being able to shed the rain well. And I know I would have missed a "Gray Ghost" Northern harrier on a very wet meadowlands morning perched on a low stump as I stumbled upon him. We looked each other in the eye, me more surprised than him. And I know for sure I would have missed that special day when an old friend joined me on a meadowlands trail as a thunderstorm came in, we grinned at each other like two mischievous schoolboys and kept birding despite it all. Someone once said, "Being soaked alone is cold. Being soaked with your best friend is an adventure."

And then, of course, there is the second method of birding in the rain. These are the mornings when despite the showers you gather your rain gear, put on your boots and hat, remember the cloth to wipe the rain drops from your binoculars and fill the thermos with hot coffee. Of course, these are the days it usually clears up and stops raining before you get out of your car. But even if it continues to sprinkle from the heavens this may be the morning when it's raining warblers and thrushes, or when you get to see a Bald eagle, feathers tussled from the constant rain fishing on the river, watch a chickadee feeding its young despite the hardships of the day or wonder at a Fox sparrow turning over the wet leaves for its next morsel of food. Despite the days when we frail humans tend to seek shelter, wildlife and our birds are still there trying to eke out a living. Nature is out there for us. No matter the weather, despite our distractions, stresses, failures, and successes, nature remains our true constant connection to the rest of world. It is our solace and our comfort, our therapist and healer, our history, and our future. Get outside and enjoy it, now more than ever before. And try a little birding in the rain, I bet it will do your heart some good.

Conversation with a Groundhog

To say the least this has been a very tough long winter for everyone. But as always seems to happen spring has finally arrived once again, and I for one could not be happier. Of course, like all nature lovers, I have been waiting impatiently for the spring invasion of warblers, the magnificence of the first Mourning Cloaks and the splendid white flowers of the Serviceberry to welcome in the season. But what I have been truly looking forward to is to continue my stimulating and thought-provoking springtime conversations with my groundhog. Yes, you heard correctly. One of my favorite spring activities is to sit in my comfy garden chair and carry on deep philosophical conversations and debates with my fuzzy backyard buddy.

The groundhogs and I discuss age old questions such as the meaning of life, national politics and sometimes even gossip about the neighbors. Groundhogs know a lot about what is going on in the neighborhood. We ramble on about our tough day at work and about our more serious family matters. We enjoy the newly emerged flowers in the garden, and they may even sample a few, just to let me know which ones they prefer. And still other times we don't talk at all, we just sit and enjoy the garden and relax. That is what good friends do sometimes.

Groundhogs are also very good listeners. I could go on and on about the events of the day and he just sits back nods his head in agreement and listens, especially if I happen to leave a strategically placed big carrot near my chair. I am not entirely sure if he really is deeply concerned about my issues, but I believe that if more people talked with groundhogs there would be very little need for the psychiatric profession ...and groundhogs don't need a referral or co-payment before they can help you out.

Now I realize there are people who like to talk with other creatures of the garden besides groundhogs. I have a friend who loves talking with trees, others with squirrels and still others think that talking with their wildflowers helps them grow. But many others love bantering with birds also. Some folks enjoy chatting with Chickadees or like to have a tête-à-tête with a Tufted Titmouse which works for them just fine. But some birds are much better conversationalist than others.

Cardinals don't hang out too long or talk much and Blue Jays just want to speak when there might be a peanut in it for them. Crows talk a lot but only to each other and Mockingbirds talk all night long. Robins just seem to eavesdrop on your conversations, and we are probably just keeping owls awake by talking too loud during the day. Mourning Doves seem to listen well, but Red-winged Blackbirds always seem like they are having too much fun to care. As for Carolina Wrens they just talk loud but not to me.

Conversing with groundhogs in my garden is one of my great pleasures. No matter what happens in the world or in my life the groundhogs, birds and butterflies are there, dependable and continuous, just as all nature is always there just waiting for us to connect to it. This spring get outside and take in all the surprises and miracles of nature and tell all the groundhogs I said hello.

I Still See Alice

In 2011, what seemed like a miracle occurred on Overpeck Creek in Ridgefield Park. What once believed to be just about impossible and could and only happen in another time and place, a pair of American Bald Eagles took up residence in one the most densely populated areas of the country. At a place no one would ever dared believe or thought even conceivable that Bald Eagles could ever survive or ever thrive, this brave pair decided they would defy the odds and make their home right here along with the rest of us. But just as soon as Alice and Al, these great symbols of our nation, became known and began their astounding comeback, they immediately came under a serious threat.

Choosing to place their nest on private property that had been slated for a multi-million-dollar development project, the powerful powers that be began to seek the proper permits to have the nest removed in the name of cleaning up a former dumping ground and in the never-ending quest for so called progress.

But as all our Bald Eagles, Alice and Al returned from the brink of extinction and struggled and fought to survive, so did the people that grew to love them fight back with the very same energy and spirit as these great birds. School children wrote letters, folks organized, good people of all ages of every political party held signs, made phone calls, signed petitions and let it be known that these Eagles would stay and no big developer, government agency or anyone else was going to tell them otherwise. And even after many people and groups said we were wasting our time and could never win, we did succeed. After a long hard struggle, Alice and Al finally won. They were allowed to stay and over the years brought forth nine more Eagles into the world to the joy and amazement of all who came to love these two amazing raptors.

In what seemed like a never-ending battle with many sleepless nights and long stressful days, people joined together to save something they felt was bigger than themselves. Like the good people that came before them that fought for the Endangered Species Act, The Clean Water and Clean Air Act that allowed the eventual return of Alice and Al, their grass roots movement showed everyone what could be done when good people choose and cared to do the right thing.

But as nature has always done and hopefully always will the circle of life has continued on even at this very special place. Life ends and is renewed and despite our best human wishes and desires, one day Alice the Eagle did not return to her nest. As everyone watched the skies and looked for the Eagle with the tracking device on her back and missing wing feather, sadly, she did not return. Even as the vigil continued, she would not be seen again gracing the skies of the Overpeck. Where had she gone? We, in all likelihood, will never know. But as in all natures glory and perfection a no less magnificent Female Eagle arrived at the nest to join up with Al to continue the magic of this most magical place.

Folks to this day including myself still look for Alice. We closely watch the skies hoping to get a glimpse of her so we can report to everyone that there is no need to worry, that she is doing fine and still patrolling the skies over her ancestral home.

But in my heart, I still see Alice. She is in the sky when we fight to save an endangered species and battle to preserve our woods and fields from destruction. I see Alice when introducing new people to nature and leading kids into the Meadowlands. I can still Alice when things seem the worst, and it feels like no one cares. Alice appears to remind me that people really do care and will stand when there seems to be no hope.

One of the last times I was blessed to see Alice the Eagle was when I was sitting at a picnic table near the Overpeck. I had just got off the phone with U.S. Fish & Wildlife Service. They gave me the news that Alice and Al's nest would be protected and there would be a 10-acre Eagle preserve built around the nest. I sat back, feeling exhausted but wonderful. With tears in my eyes, I looked up and there was Alice! She was cruising very low right over my table. I could see her tracking device and her missing wing feather, and in my most human way I felt she may have been saying thank you. Thanks for protecting us and standing up for us, and now, it seems, she may have been also saying goodbye.

Alice still soars with all of us when we need her most. When we think we have done all we can do, when we think we are too tired to continue on, Alice is there to remind us what we can do when we all join together to stand up for what is right. She will always be there, just look up and you will see her too.

Even a Snake Needs a Good Home

Last week I was doing some yard work, getting my garden ready for the hummingbirds and butterflies that I had faith would visit my tiny backyard this summer. As I was planting, weeding, and performing some basic garden chores, I was suddenly startled by a small slithering surprise that was hiding in a small flowerpot which still held some soil from the previous year. A Brown Snake! It was a wonderful sight to behold, especially since it had been many years since I enjoyed the pleasure of having one of these lovely creatures grace my backyard. As it glided into the underbrush of my backyard wilderness, I had a feeling of reprieve that this tiny creature still managed to survive the onslaught of suburban life.

For a young boy growing up in the Meadowlands searching for snakes was a rite of passage. Garter, Milk and Brown Snakes occupied many of our summer days as we explored the woods and marshes of our meadowlands home. As I grew up, I came to understand how important snakes were to our environment and how my backyard inhabitant the Northern Brown Snake was keeping my garden healthy and in balance.

Northern Brown Snakes (DeKay's Snake) are small harmless, nonvenomous and avoid humans whenever they can. They are very docile and although they can produce musk and sometimes bite if handled, it is very rare. They have a deep brown body and two rows of darker spots along its back. Its belly is gray to pink and can have small black spots. They can grow to be 9 to 15 inches long. Brown Snakes are very shy, mostly solitary and spend most of their lives underground or under cover. They are most active at night, particularly during the summer. They feed largely on earthworms, snails, and slugs, but will also eat small grubs, and beetles, some of which are considered garden pests.

Sadly, Northern Brown Snakes are very susceptible to backyard pesticides, insecticides and lawn chemicals which is why they have become a rare sight in some areas of our New Jersey suburban neighborhoods. They also very often fall victim to human misunderstanding and are killed off due to fear and ignorance. My former neighbor would kill them and show them to me, as if he was doing a good thing. My constant attempts to explain to him why they were good for his garden fell on deaf ears. His recent departure however could be why this great little snake has returned to my Meadowlands backyard.

You can help the Northern Brown Snake by keeping a healthy organic chemical free backyard. Eliminating the use of any harmful chemicals in the garden is crucial if you want to attract and keep the Brown snakes among others healthy in your garden. Going organic is not only better for you and the environment but also for all life in the garden. Harsh fertilizers and herbicides can also harm snakes and will eliminate their food source.

Keeping a healthy place for all our creatures including snakes will help keep our suburban backyards in in balance with nature and make a better environment for all of us to live.

Chat with a Hummingbird

By now anyone that has read my essays over the years or for that matter wanders the woods and meadows with me knows I like to talk to wildlife. I have had in depth and detailed conversations with everything from bears to bumble bees and beavers to butterflies. These days it seems that it has just become an automatic response that I immediately greet the creatures I meet along the way on my daily adventures from my backyard garden to the Meadowlands. Maybe it's just that I am getting older that I don't really care who hears me or worry about the strange looks I get from folks that don't know the pleasure of conversing with natures creatures. Some of the best conversations I have had have been with a groundhog in my backyard named Chucky that was well versed on any topic I chose to speak about. He was also an excellent listener and agreed with me just about all the time especially if I happened to have a nice big carrot in my hand.

I also love to stop and talk with a very large Draft horse named "Smalls" on my way our butterfly garden at the Bergen Equestrian Center. No matter what is going on that day, Smalls always has the time to come over to the fence and reach over for a morning hello, a scratch on the nose and a nod of his head as he listens to my plans for the day ahead. It is a perfect way to start the day in my book. I believe if more people took the time to talk with the wildlife and all animals for that matter, it may limit our visits to the psychologist's couch. Although there are people that think talking to animals should make our search for medical care more frequent, but obviously they never have spoken to a Red-tailed Hawk or a Monarch Butterfly.

Now last Thursday I had a very important and in depth talk with a Ruby-throated Hummingbird. I didn't plan the chat but as life has it, I had a tough morning. On my way to our butterfly garden, I was involved in a four-car accident. No one was seriously hurt but I did have to help someone get out of a badly smashed car, not the way I wanted to start my day. Fortunately, my truck and myself were lucky and not much worse for wear. Sitting along the roadside after all was said and done, I didn't know whether to just go home or continue on my original destination and get some work done at the garden. Of course, I chose the most therapeutic place to visit I could think of, a social call with Mother Nature.

Walking into the garden I was immediately greeted by a beautiful male Ruby-throated Hummingbird prancing around on the honeysuckle. He didn't seem frightened at all, rather more curious. Without thinking I just blurted out, "Good Morning sir, how are you today?" The hummer still didn't flinch and just hovered at eye level just a few feet away, obviously to see if I had anything more important to say. I didn't think he would care much about human stuff like cars, insurance, or tough days. After all this tiny little guy was headed south, a journey much more arduous and dangerous than even a New Jersey highway.

I continued our conversation, asked him how he was, mentioned that I much appreciated him visiting our butterfly garden this morning, hoped he had enough to eat to continue his travels, and wished him Godspeed and a safe journey ahead. The Hummer darted quickly around my head. He hovered up, down and sideways. Then he looked at me again and went right back to sipping nectar from our flowers as quickly as it could.

As I slowly sat back in the garden chair and observed this surreal magical bird drift from flower to flower, it made the events of the day seem much less important. I knew I would soon have to face the trials and tribulations of daily life as soon as I left the garden but for this special moment in time, none of that mattered much. Being in nature helps us realize that there is something bigger than ourselves. Things that have existed since time began continue on with not much regard for our very human made frailties. And yet coming to that realization helps all of us to better understand who we truly are and how we fit into the natural world just like the little hummer that took a few minutes of his busy day to at least pretend to give a listen to what I had to say.

Stopping once in a while to take in nature and say a simple hello or good morning to the creatures we share our Earth with can help better connect us to nature and reminds us we are not alone in our struggle to survive. And besides, it just might be the perfect way to start a new day by recognizing the life that thrives and fights to survive day to day just as we do.

The Promise of Spring

No matter where you live you can open your door and hear the Robins, Cardinals and Song Sparrows singing their spring song as they have done for eons past. A closer look and you will see the new tiny yellow flowers of the Spicebush and buds on the Serviceberry preparing for the reemergence and renewal of life of the season ahead. The Osprey has returned, and the Tree Swallow hopes for our help as it searches for its special nesting place to raise its family once again.

During this pandemic, as we hunker down at home with our families and experience fears and anxiety that we have never known in our generation, nature is continuing. Despite our very human frailties, our new limitations and our lives altered, nature continues to endure, unafraid and uninhibited. It is all around us just waiting for us to give a glance and pay some notice and let it know that we are aware of its eternal existence. Not that nature needs us but rather, its patiently waiting for us with the song of a Wood Thrush or the sight of a wildflower to realize we are as much part of nature as all the wild creatures that endure to survive each and every day.

Over the last week of this pandemic, I have seen more and more people craving nature and walking the fields and woodlands of our local nature centers and parks. What seems like a long time ago just a few weeks back we were begging everyone to get away from their phones and computers and get outside and now there is no need to urge them to seek out nature. We all now realize, instinctively that we need nature to heal our pain and soothe our souls.

We still have a way to go before we come out on the other side but make no mistake we will. With great tragedy comes great understanding and now we have come to appreciate or rather been harshly reminded of how much we really need each other how important nature is to have in our lives. It is my hope that we never forget either of these important lessons and we begin a new and better relationship with the natural world and each other.

Gardening Like Life Depends on It

For generations home gardeners have literally changed the ecosystems of our neighborhoods and unfortunately not for the better. Where once native trees, shrubs and flowers stood now have been replaced by plants from other places around the world, creating a false habitat; one that looks lush and inviting but is insidiously void of the needed life support for our birds and butterflies.

Years ago, this may not have been so important to the natural scheme of things. But as more and more land was sacrificed for commercial development and urban sprawl, the habitat that was left became fragmented and invaded by the very same plants that we unwittingly introduced into our home gardens. These plants outcompete our native plants and are of no value to the wildlife that is depending on them. Simply speaking, when a migratory bird stops in your backyard looking for a meal and it is full of non-native plants, they may have just as well landed in a yard of plastic artificial flowers; appealing to the eye but when examined closer is totally void of sustaining life as we know it.

Can the bird move on? Well maybe, if it still has the strength to move on and if there is somewhere else to actually go to before there is any food to be found. Imagine if you are a species of warbler traveling hundreds of miles through many hazardous nights and totally out of the ability to continue the arduous journey without sustenance, and you land in a yard chock full of plants that have no benefit to you. This could very well be the last stop on your journey.

How and why did we get away from our native plants and instead choose plants from foreign places? Some of it may have to do with folks collecting plants the way we do baseball cards. But I also think somewhere along line we were convinced that insects were not allowed in our yards. If we noticed even a pinhole in a leaf we had to bring home toxic chemicals to kill them. And then to make sure we buy plants that the garden center told us did not even attract insects. This notion of misunderstanding and fear has helped us lose 3 billion birds since 1970.

Our native plants get their flowers, seeds, and berries at exactly the right time our wildlife needs them and with exactly the right nutritional value. But often overlooked is the fact that the insects that are attracted to the plants are the most important part of the puzzle. They are the lifeblood of the ecosystem and the native plants themselves are the very foundation that holds that ecosystem together.

Whether it is your backyard Cardinal or Chickadee, they need insects to bring forth the next generation. A Black capped Chickadee may collect 400 caterpillars a day or more to feed its young. High protein, high fat insects are the perfect food for raising babies. Without them, nests will fail, and the next generation of birds will not and cannot exist. If you have nesting birds in your yard watch them closely. From sunup to sundown the parent birds go back and forth carrying insects to their young.

If the plants are not there that attract those insects the young will not survive. This is not to say that if you plant natives that you will have insects swarming in your back yard. It's quite the opposite. When the ecology of your backyard is restored, all things will be in balance once again, everything keeping everything else in check. Why don't you see lightning bugs any longer or incredible creatures like Luna moths? The answer is the way we garden, against nature rather than with it.

Our butterflies have suffered as well from the introduction of non-native plants into the home landscape. Butterfly populations are very specific to the plants they need to survive. Milkweed for the Monarchs, Spicebush for the Spicebush Swallowtail and Violets for the Fritillaries. We cannot substitute non-natives and expect to see the butterflies like we did years ago.

We can longer pretend we care about birds if we continue to plant things like Bradford Pear Trees, which attract 0 species of Lepidoptera (moths and butterflies) as compared to an Oak tree that attracts over 400! We do not have the luxury of saying we care about butterflies if we are planting things like invasive daylilies and avoid wildflowers like Milkweed, Joe-Pye weed and Goldenrods.

We now know we need to garden differently and treat our backyards, schoolyards, churches, and businesses like they are habitats if we are to save the future of our wildlife. We are irresponsible if we continue to introduce toxins into our gardens while advocating for a healthy environment for both wildlife and people. Sadly, if we received notice that our elected officials were treating our parks the way we treat our backyards, we would be out in the streets with protest signs demanding a halt to the environment's mistreatment. When we realize that everything in the natural world is connected and that our backyards are the strong link that now bring it together, we will begin to live in a happier, more healthy life sustaining place not only for the Monarch butterfly and the Northern cardinal but for all the human species for generations to come.

Changing the culture of how we gardened for generations may be the most difficult task of all. But if we fail to do that, we will continue to witness a decline of bird and butterfly species that will be too late to halt. When we walk into our backyards from now on, I hope we can begin to look at things in a new light. We will understand that a hole in a leaf means that things are as they should be, that a garter snake slinking through the flower bed means you are doing something right and a house wren carrying a caterpillar back to the bird house you so kindly placed there for them means that the cycle of life is as it should and was always meant to be. Ecology begins at home, and we need to garden like life depends on it. Because it absolutely does.

In Common Milkweed, Life Abounds

I once read an article that said more was known about nature in the tropical rain forest than the life that exists in your own backyard. I am not sure if that is true, but I do know if you were to take a closer look at a patch of Common Milkweed that lies in the vacant lot down the street or behind your house you may be extremely amazed at the life that flourishes there.

Common Milkweed (Asclepias syriaca) is the Rodney Dangerfield of plants. It gets no respect, no respect at all. You may find it growing along roadsides, railroad tracks, fields and even your backyard. It has large, broad leaves, usually four to ten inches long and the beautiful flowers are pinkish-purple clusters which fill the air with a wonderful vanilla or honey scent. I grow Common Milkweed right in my front yard and passersby often ask me what that beautiful flower is. I never say Milkweed. I say its "Asclepias" not wanting to be accused by local authorities of growing so called "weeds" in my front yard. Unfortunately, Common Milkweed is usually the innocent victim of spraying, mowing and just being cut down. Common Milkweed is often considered a plant that just gets in the way, which in the end can be catastrophic to many species of wildlife that depend on it for survival.

We should all know by now that the Monarch Butterfly's very existence depends on milkweed. The milkweed species is the only plant that the majestic Monarch Butterfly will lay its eggs on. No Milkweed, no Monarchs, it is that simple. But what most people are not aware of is that there are many other species of animals that have come to depend on the Common Milkweed for their survival too.

Besides the Monarch, Milkweed Bugs and Milkweed Leaf Beetles only eat milkweed and although those species may seem trivial, they play an important part in the ecosystem that has evolved around the milkweed. Many other butterfly species depend on the milkweed flowers. Eastern Tiger Swallowtails, Great Spangled Fritillaries and Painted Ladies are just a few of the butterflies that love to partake of the nectar that the beautiful pink orbs produce.

Many pollinators such as Bumble Bees and Honeybees are attracted to Common Milkweed like a mystical floral magnet. Many moth species such as Hummingbird and Sphinx moths find milkweed irresistible. And let's not forget the predators such as the Black and Yellow Argiope and the Goldenrod Crab Spider that depend on the milkweed for continuing their lifecycle. Mammals live among the milkweeds also like the White-footed Mouse and the Eastern Mole and reptiles like the Brown and Garter Snakes find good hunting among the milkweeds. And please let us not forget how important Common Milkweed is to the birds. Among the many avian creatures of the air that utilize Common Milkweed are the Barn and Tree Swallows that love to soar through the milkweed and snatch up its bounty of insects. Yellow Warblers, Common Yellowthroat and House Wrens love the tasty little insects' morsels that are so important to their survival. Not to mention our Robins, Catbirds and Orioles find the milkweed so valuable. And we should not be surprised when we see how much the Ruby-Throated Hummingbird relishes the nectar of the milkweed.

Due to modern farming practices and genetically engineered crops that allow farmers to use more weed killing chemicals such as Round-up, less Common milkweed can be found in the wild. Additionally, urbanization and homeowners digging out milkweed in favor of non-native exotic plants has become commonplace. It causes a serious problem for the wildlife that depends on this incredible life-giving plant.

Among the milkweed that lies in and about your neighborhood exists a unique and wondrous ecosystem, although it may occur along the roadside, next to an old warehouse or on the fringes of parks and golf courses it is no less an important bionetwork than the rainforest. If you are lucky enough to have a large stand of milkweed nearby, pull up a chair and watch for a while. The creatures that thrive there will give you a whole new perspective on what makes an ecosystem.

Standing up and preserving stands of milkweed at our local parks, schoolyards and nature centers is vitally important to a healthy environment. We all need to relearn and educate each other on what a healthy and vital habitat really means. Growing milkweed in our backyards and conserving our Common Milkweed around our neighborhood is a good place to start.

Give Wildlife a Break

As we rise again from the tragedy of Covid19, we can look back and remember all the news reports on how wildlife was enjoying a much-needed vacation from us. Birds, mammals whatever wildlife hid under our porch, laid low in the woods, or otherwise left the area entirely seemed to come back and enjoy the time they without our constant interference.

As conservationists and nature lovers we are all very much concerned about the future of our birds and of course all of our wildlife. Climate change, habitat loss and pollution top the list of issues that keep us up at night worrying if future generations will get to enjoy nature the way we have.

But at the same time, I see things that many folks do every day that just seems to turn a blind eye to the wildlife that tries so very hard every day to survive right around our own neighborhoods. Somehow, we have managed to disconnect ourselves from the rest of the world believing that what we do at home does not affect the overall ecosystem. But, in reality, it very much does. And the future of many species may ultimately depend on how we conduct ourselves in and around our own backyard. So, if you are ready for a little tough love please continue reading.

I am often saddened on how little tolerance homeowners have for nesting birds. If there is a bird nest near their front door or on a window ledge they want it moved or just out of there ASAP. We could give a nesting bird a break by being a little more easy-going and letting them raise its young that it fought so very hard to do in the first place. After all it will only be a few weeks and then the birds will be gone. Nature should teach us patience and being a little inconvenienced once in a while is not always a bad thing especially when it comes to giving nature a helping hand. It can be a magnificent family experience of watching nestlings go out into the world for the first time.

We could also give all wildlife a break by stopping the pesticide and insecticide uses in our backyards. If you got a call from your local town and they told you they were going to spray pesticides everywhere, you would run down to borough hall with a picket sign. And yet we think nothing of using these toxins all around our homes. Then of course we wonder why we don't see bees, butterflies and birds like we used to. Often poisons can be avoided to solve a problem and when all things are in balance most garden pets take care of themselves. So please, Go Organic! No one will call you an old hippie, in the end its just about the health of our families and our community.

If I had a dollar for every bird I rescued over the years that was caught in fishing line, I would be writing this column from the Galapagos. Birds and other wildlife suffer a terrible death from fishing line if they are not found and rescued and most times they are not. Recently, we sadly had to recover a Great Horned Owl that was strangled to death on fishing line that was left on a tree. Clean up your line and if you see line on the ground even if it is not yours, please pick it up, very often there are fishing line recovery bins along lakes and ponds, is it a little inconvenient? Sure, but the alternative is far worse.

And while we are at it, please resist the temptation to release balloons! They kill wildlife such as turtles and birds every day. There are much better ways to celebrate events than doing something that kills so many living creatures and if you are like me, you never want to see another photo of a dead animal with a balloon in its throat or tangled around its feet.

This is a tough one for some of you I know, but if you care anything about the future of our bird populations, please keep your cat indoors. They are not wild creatures. They are not part of our ecosystem, and they kill millions of birds each year. I heard all the excuses and none of them hold water. Love your cat? Please keep it safe indoors.

Bird deaths from window strikes is out of control but we only think of big office buildings and skyscrapers of being the culprit, but our homes can be just as deadly. There are many solutions including putting up decals especially made for preventing this kind of tragedy. We can't very well ask corporations to help if we don't do something ourselves at home.

My last plea of the day will really get some of you very upset with me but let me ask you a big favor. Please try to be more tolerant of the creatures that roam your backyard like the groundhogs, squirrels, and possums. They are only trying to survive and unfortunately in many cases the last places they have to survive is our suburban neighborhoods. When I hear some of the awful things people do to these poor animals, it is heartbreaking. Maybe consider putting out a few extra tomato plants and setting aside part of your garden that you can share with some of our woodland friends, after all it might just go a long way to teaching our kids and grandchildren to be more tolerant of the natural world around them. There are also some positive things you can do to help:

Use Native Plants in the backyard! Everything from birds to butterflies depends on our native plants to survive. Creating a small habitat can help birds endure the stresses of climate change and bring back many of our butterfly and pollinator species that we are losing every year.

Put out some water! Many of the ponds and streams we played in as kids no longer exist. By putting out a simple bird bath or even just a shallow tray of water it will help migratory birds as they continue their long arduous journey along the flyway. Just change the water often so not to get mosquitos and all will be fine for all concerned.

Put up some Bird houses. Just about everyone can put up a bird house somewhere. There is a housing shortage in New Jersey not only for people but for birds too. Bird houses will help everything from Chickadees, Wrens and even Owls raise their families and bring forth the next generation of the birds we love so much.

Put up a bird feeder! I understand this is not for everyone and I realize there is an expense plus many people live in places where it is not practical or possible to feed the birds. But if you can feeders will help birds survive migration and nesting season and especially help through severe cold and wet winters. And one of my favorite things about feeders is that they help folks connect more with nature which is always important. Keep the feeders and the ground clean and use a good healthy bird seed mix. AND PLEASE do not feed birds bread! It is the ultimate junk food filling their stomachs with material that has no nutritional value whatsoever.

Take a child birding. One moment in nature may create a lifelong passion for the outdoors and thereby helping to make the world a better place for wildlife and humankind also.

We very much need to change our way of thinking when it comes to wildlife in our community. A little bit of tolerance, patience, understanding and education will help us not to be so hard on the wildlife that wants the same things as all of us, to be safe, have a good meal, and to successfully bring forth their next generation. So whenever and wherever you can let's try our best give wildlife a break, it's the very least we can do.

Tribute to Alice the Eagle

In 2011, a pair of American Bald Eagles nested the most unlikely of places. Amid the concrete, cars, and steel of the most densely populated state inside the most highly populated county, a species once thought lost forever had the tenacity and stubbornness to try and raise a family in place once believed to be impossible. And yet they not only survived but thrived in an urban wilderness not very welcoming to wild creatures.

Alice and Al as these two magnificent symbols of our nation became known, were named after Alice Leurck and her husband Al, as she was the first person the photograph "Alice the Eagle" during a Bergen Audubon field trip at Overpeck park back in 2010. As the battle to preserve and protect Alice's nest from a multi-million-dollar development project unfolded, they soon became a symbol and the line in the sand to defend urban endangered species that decided to take up residence amongst its human neighbors.

Over the years Alice has produced nine eagles from one of the most urbanized nests in the country. Nine more Eagles were sent into the wild to help continue the comeback of a species that has fought back from the brink of extinction. This is an accomplishment that should never be taken for granted and always to be admired and held up for all to see of what can be accomplished when a species is given a chance to survive.

This season started differently than in past years. An agreement by developers to preserve Alice and Al's home as an Eagle Park gave everyone a sense of relief and accomplishment. And as a record number of Eagles began to gather around the nest site on the Overpeck, it confirmed our long-time argument that this area was critical not only to nesting eagles but also as an important Bald Eagle wintering habitat which deserved equal protection. But as nesting time approached, and everyone anticipated another successful season it was soon realized Alice the Eagle was nowhere to be found. We also soon came to see that she had been replaced by a new larger female now taking up residence in her long-time nest.

As much as I dreaded and denied it, I knew this day would have to come. An Eagles life is full of threats and everyday dangers. From the hazards of urban life from electric wires, cars, and trucks to competition from other Eagles contending for prime nesting areas and mates. Alice was at least 13 years old, getting up there for a wild bald eagle. Was she driven off? Did she meet with an untimely death? We may never know. But what we do know for sure Alice the Eagle will never be forgotten.

Alice was and is a symbol of hope for not only hard-core conservationist but also for the everyday person that understood that something special happened right in their neighborhood. As the morning commutes took place and millions moved to the jobs and schools there were nesting Bald Eagles in suburban Bergen County, among the tension, sprawl, and stress of life in Jersey something happened never thought possible. A sight not witnessed in many generations was now seen by all in a tribute to what can be accomplished when good people care enough and work together to do the right thing.

We are not theoretically supposed to be concerned over an individual wild creature but rather our focus, we are told, should always be on the overall health of the species. But while our brain tells us one thing our hearts tell us quite another, we missed Alice.

This is not to in any way to diminish the importance of this new Eagle pair. They are just as magnificent and should be equally cherished because they helped prove what a prolific and vital an Eagle habitat the Overpeck is. They will be looked at in just as much awe and wonder and be fought for just as hard as any bald Eagle pair ever has, that is without question. But Alice, after all, was the first and there will always something extraordinary and unforgettable about that.

I want to believe that Alice still flies wild, that somewhere she is catching fish and giving people a thrill of a lifetime that is honored to see a Bald Eagle for the very first time. I know that Alice will never be forgotten by anyone who had the delight and privilege of watching her grace the skies of the Overpeck. Alice gave us a reason to stand together for what was right and gave us the strength to understand that anything is possible because Eagles

now fly once more in our heart and hometown.
Godspeed, Alice, wherever you are.

Above all, Always Stay Curious

"What's inside that flower Mr. Don?" a little girl asked me as we walked around our butterfly garden. We both stared together into a large white hibiscus with a pink center. I honestly could not remember when I last looked that long or closely into a flower. My fascination got the better of me and when I didn't answer right away, she looked back at me with her big curious eyes and said, "well?"

Without going into the detailed anatomy of the flower (which I am not sure I totally remember anyway), I quickly explained this was where pollination happens and that is how the plants make more seeds to get more plants. She looked up at me again after staring what felt like forever back into the flower. "WOW! That is COOL," she said grinning ear to ear and walked down the trail to join the other kids in the garden... Yes, I thought to myself, how very, very cool for sure.

I came to realize many years ago that for some unexplained reason there just some people that are not interested in the natural world. If a Bald Eagle came down and sat on their heads and built a nest, they would just go on ignoring the falling sticks and fish bones that fell around their feet every day. And just so you know I have in no way given up on those folks just yet.

But at the same time, I also discovered there is one very important thing that unifies everyone that cares about and loves nature. Whether it is that young girl in the garden staring into the flower or scientists working on long term solutions for the environment, it is curiosity. It is the very same childhood curiosity that gives all of them the desire and drive to learn more and forever be fascinated and connected with the wonders of the natural world. In fact, as I was writing this column, I saw on the news a curious 4-year-old girl in Palo Alto found a species of stingless bee that no one has seen in more than 70 years. Now they will name the little bee after her, the Anika Bee. We never know where and how far that magical kind curiosity will take us.

Still, today, my first steps into the woods and meadows brings me right back to my childhood curiosity and the many questions that I still search for. Yes, maybe more detailed than my 10-year-old self-had back in the day but still I wonder why do birds migrate? Where do butterflies go in winter? And for that matter why is the sky blue or sometimes not so much anymore? These questions still push me up the next trail and down a future winding path.

It is my hope that despite life's ups and downs, triumphs, and tragedies, we never lose that curiosity that allowed us to love our first Cardinal or get chills when we saw our first Eagle. Let's not let the news of the day, concerns of the future or dissenting disagreement get in the way of wondering how we can help a Monarch, stop climate change, or save a stand of trees in your own neighborhood. Then maybe as our curiosity expands our view of the world it will also bring us closer together in a better understanding on how dependent we are on each other.

Stephen Hawking once said, "Remember to look up at the stars and not down at your feet. Try to make sense of what you see and wonder about what makes the universe exist. Be curious. And however difficult life may seem, there is always something you can do and succeed at. It matters that you don't just give up."

Red Admiral Butterfly at Dekorte

Eastern Tiger Swallowtail Butterfly

Least Sandpiper, the smallest shorebird

Lesser Yellowlegs on the mudflats

Life with Birds

Not a single day goes by that I don't get a phone call, text, or email about how a bird is in some way is enriching someone's life. It may be that a bird they have never seen before shows up at a backyard feeder, or it maybe about a family member that has passed on is being thought about when that special Cardinal appears to reassure them that all will be fine.

It might be the life changing event of seeing a 'life bird' the one that never leaves you, that stays in your heart and soul forever, the bird that goes with you everywhere on your journey. It might be the first bird your child saw on one of your first time walks through the woods and meadows or even the very last time you and a friend enjoyed the birds together that still holds that special place in your heart.

From Native Americans' belief that the Eagle is the messenger to the Great Spirit to the symbol of the Dove in Christianity, from ancient cave drawings of birds to the paintings of Audubon, Peterson and Sibley. Birds, no matter if you are an avid birder or the person that just happens to notice a bird flying overhead on the way to work. There is no denying our birds have enriched our everyday lives and made them better at least in some small way.

Maybe because I am getting up there in years, I tend to think about my own life journey with the birds as much as I do about the birds themselves. At times I think we might get lost in the lists, the Apps and the species race and not realize how much of our life's adventures and journey is connected to our passion for birds and nature. Through life's ups and downs, good times and bad, the birds have always been there for me. No matter what was happening in the world around me, I could always count on the birds to sooth my soul and renew my spirit. Births and deaths, tragedy, and celebration those times are intertwined in my heart and memories forever along with my first Bald Eagle and the joy of birding with good friends. To let these things go by without a thought, would be like turning away from a rare bird without a glance, something that should never ever be done.

Perhaps it was the special place you stopped, the good folks you met and the birds you found along your birding highway. Maybe it was the rain, the laughs, or even the sadness that brought you to where you were with the birds. Sometimes like life, a birding journey can't be planned or anticipated rather it's better to let it happen and just enjoy the unforgettable ride. No matter how much we try nature and life cannot be controlled and that is the way it should be.

Our Lives are all about journey and the stories we recollect. Especially from the days when we could run full all-out day and night without rest to the years when things slowed down, and our life's sagas became more about old friends and family. These are the times we love to recall when we have big audiences and the stories we love to remember when we are sitting on the front porch alone. They are the stories we love to pass on to our children and our grandchildren and the stories we use to remind all our old buddies about where we have been and what we have done. They are our stories, the ones we hold deep in our hearts and save in that very special place to bring out when we need a smile or to renew our souls. And for bird lovers the stories can sometimes mean even more.

It is my hope that we all can make birds a part of our lives and never ever have to know or even imagine what it may be like to ever have a life without birds.

Good Morning from A Fish Crow

It seems just about every morning as I head out the door for work there is a Fish Crow perched atop a nearby telephone pole voicing its nasally call for the all the world to hear. Although I am usually rushing to my truck dreading the coming onslaught of the morning route 17 traffic, I try to stop and give my corvid friend a hello back. "Hey up there," I usually yell out not caring much if my neighbors look at me a little strangely (I rarely say good morning to them). Of course, the crow never pays me any mind at all. Kind of rude but then again, I am sure he or she is having a very busy morning also.

I became well aware of how the Fish Crow has been expanding its range and becoming my welcome but noisy neighbor during hurricane Sandy. For days as the flood waters around my house receded, the Fish Crows had a feast on all the fish that sadly wound up stranded in the streets and backyards. Bad for the fish but the motherload for the friends and family of my pole sitting town crier. For that matter there are even a flock of Fish Crows hanging around my place of employment on route 17 in Paramus on a daily basis. Not sure what they are doing there but at least they don't get delayed at route 4 on the way home the way I do.

The Corvid family of birds including Jays, Crows, and Ravens are legendary as far as their intelligence goes. Some say they take care of their injured and elderly and sometimes even seem to mourn the dead. We might all take a lesson from them.

Although I may be unique in my thinking, I consider my Fish Crow friends and for that matter most any wildlife just as much a part of the place where I have chosen to live as anyone or anything else that attempts to call my neighborhood their home... After all, they are with us every day if you choose just to look up, take a glance, and just pay some attention. They are there when we are on the way to work, at school and in bed. Our wildlife much like us is out there every day trying their best to find enough food, raise their young and be safe. These are the same things we are all striving for day in and day out our whole lives.

So the next time a Fish crow, a Chickadee or even the neighborhood squirrel takes the time to greet you, say hello, good morning and Godspeed, after all we are neighbors and are all in this together.

The Suburban Conservationist

Our historical idea of the great American conservationist conjures up iconic images of John Muir Hiking in the High Sierras, Teddy Roosevelt on horseback on the Western plains and Rachel Carson bringing attention to the environmental disaster of DDT. All those environmental heroes and many more still very much inspire, motivate and at times give many of us the inner strength to continue on the daily stresses and strains of looking after an environment placed between concrete and cars. But today, the conservationist in suburbia and especially here in northern New Jersey has a very different job. It's one that is a much less glamourous and newsworthy but at the same time no less crucial and critical to the wildlife and the people of the communities where they live.

As the battle to hold back climate change, save endangered species, and preserve places in the Artic and the rain forest goes on all around us, my day usually begins with phone calls and texts of an injured raptor just hit by a car, a local town threatening to mow down a stand of milkweed , a call from NJDEP concerning a local endangered species or something as simple as can I identify a bird in the backyard, just to name a few.

Now I have to admit there are many days that are very frustrating and down right depressing especially when it seems that there are so many important issues going on all around us. A local town wants to take down trees, birds are hitting glass windows at an office building, and a construction project is ready for the bulldozers to roll. Which fight do you take up? As we all know, or maybe not, conservation organizations have limited resources and picking your battles is a daily decision which can easily cause one to hang one's head in surrender. At times suburban conservation is like a firefighter having to decide which blaze to put out first in hopes that the others don't get out of control before you can get to them or if you can at all.

But, of course, there are those wonderfully magical times that make it all worth it when you get to do something you know will have an impact on the community that will last for generations. Saving an Eagles nest in a suburban town, winning a fight to preserving a local wildlife habitat, creating butterfly gardens, showing a child their first Monarch Butterfly and putting out nest boxes, all to help our wildlife through the trials and tribulations of suburban life. And all this has to be done with little money, no lawyers at your fingertips and yes entirely with a staff of hard-working volunteers ...and I am proud to say would not have it any other way.

I have had the distinct honor of showing someone their first hummingbird, holding a peregrine falcon in my hand, digging holes for new milkweed plants, and yes when needed standing up for what needs to be done to protect wildlife where it chooses to be, not where the powers that be think it should be.

Now some well-meaning folks will say that fighting to preserve open space and protect wildlife in suburbia is not that important and that our resources would do better to focus on bigger places and bigger issues in other places. But, at least, to me that is an old and destructive way of looking at the environment and puts nature and wildlife in a box in can never get out of.

Today we better understand how important both the suburban and urban habitat is to migratory birds, butterflies and pollinators. It creates not only much needed breeding areas but critical steppingstones for migratory birds, birds that will never get to those vaster habitats unless the ones in suburbia are saved also. I don't believe we have to decide on one or the other, we can do both, fight for the bigger picture and still preserve and protect nature at the local level. In reality, we will have no choice but to accomplish both.

Our responsibilities as local conservationists are vast and diverse and take on jobs such as monitoring local endangered species, leading nature walks, educating school children, helping to create backyard wildlife habitats, and working with local communities and governments' on how to do the right thing when it comes to the natural outdoors. It's much different than the idea of wandering a wilderness and looking into the sunset.

Make no mistake. The big more visible national environmental campaigns are as important than ever, maybe even more so. But it's also important that we don't forget that conservation begins at home. And although very different and unique Suburban conservation needs to be stepped up and find new ways to be sure even in both urban and suburban environments that the wildlife and the people live in place where they can lead happy and healthy lives for many years to come.

I Talk to Birds

I was leading a field trip a while back and a cheerful little Chickadee flew up onto a branch an inch from my nose. Without thinking I blurted out a "Good morning to you," as the tiny little bird tilted its head and gazed at me with what seemed to be a somewhat puzzled look. That's when I heard giggling from the woman behind me, "What's the matter, don't you talk to the birds I asked?" She just continued to chuckle. I forgot for a second there was a line of folks trailing behind me waiting for me to point out a life bird or give them some brilliant insight into the wonders of nature. But instead, I was greeting a little bird like it was my neighbor gesturing to me from across the driveway or like waving to the guy letting me merge into traffic on route 17 in the morning. I looked around quickly to see if anyone else heard my avian salutation and trusted they didn't think there was a possible "Silver Alert" out for me. After all I was supposed to be the leader. And although nature lovers are legendary in their eccentricities, I didn't want everyone thinking I was one acorn away from the nut farm.

Now I do confess, I have been known at times, at least when I think no one is watching, to have heart to hearts with Hummingbirds, dialog with Mourning Doves, raps with Wrens, chats with Chats, and parleys with Palm warblers and, for God's sake don't tell the birds, words of wisdom with Woodchucks and sometimes even soliloquies with the Squirrels.

Animals seem to be very good listeners. I could sit in my lawn chair and go on and on all day about politics, world affairs and they always seem to agree with me no matter how far reaching my opinions may be. The Little Downy Woodpecker on my suet feeder just keeps pecking away while I tell tales about the day's events. I am not sure if they really care about what I have to say. I like to think they are at least a little interested, but they are always very polite and nod their heads in agreement on occasion. Besides I think talking with the local wildlife has saved me a fortune in therapy bills.   But I often wonder, am I the only one who babbles with the birds? My fears were soon put at ease.

Cathy wrote to me to say, "I say good morning to the Cardinal that sings in my yard every day. Such beautiful birds! Just the sight of them makes me smile." A good a reason as any to say hello as I can see it!

Cardinals seem to be on the top of the list for conversations as far as my good friend, Marie, is concerned, "I have a male Cardinal in my area and if he hears me open the window on the side of our house he comes flying over to the window I say, 'Good Morning,' handsome and he takes the peanut before the squirrel can get to it. But I talk to them all. I think someone someday is going to report me to the proper authorities!"

Lisa takes communicating with her birds a step further, "I sing to them. Oh, I wish I Was in Dixie, or the Skye Boat Song - I was trying to teach the latter to the baby Carolina

Wrens nesting in my oven exhaust fan duct (it does not seem to have worked). Just trying to find a way to communicate! "

Julie has come clean about her encounters of the avian kind. "I do sometimes talk to the birds. Granted, many of these conversations are one-sided, and consist mainly of comments such as, 'Look at you! Hello, gorgeous!' and even more frequently, 'Where are you?' and 'Come back here...'"

So, what is it that makes us speak to the birds? Is it some ancient yearning we have to be closer to nature? Or maybe it's a kind of a hopeful wish that they will let us into their world even for just that brief second when we say, "Good morning to you little bird."

If we have enough reverence for our feathered friends to give them a special greeting when we are privileged enough to come upon them, then I think they should be respected enough that we can endure some minor inconveniences such as using the back door so not to disturb the nesting Robins over your front door. Don't grumble so much when there is a little bird poop on the car, after all that is why God made rain and most important as inconvenient and as difficult as it can be at times, we need to stand up and protect the patch of woods down the street , the pond around the corner and all their habitat when it is threatened in and around your neighborhood and all over New Jersey. After all, it's the least we can do for the creatures we love to talk to everyday.

Our Birding Stories

Our lives are all about stories, the stories we recollect from the days when we could run full out day and night without rest to the years when things slowed down, and our life's sagas became more about old friends and family. These are the very same tales we love to recall when we have big audiences and the stories we love to remember when we are sitting on the front porch alone. They are the stories we love to pass on to our children and our Grandchildren and the stories we use to remind all our old buddies about where we have been and what we have done. They are our stories, the ones we hold deep in our hearts and save in that very special place to bring out when we need a smile or to renew our souls. And for birders the stories can sometimes mean even more.

Just as in life, birding is all about the stories too. Our stories are about the time when we saw our first Hummingbird buzz by your nose and felt the breeze from its wings on your cheek. They are stories that tell how you thought your heart was going to jump out of your chest when you watched your first Eagle soar overhead. They are the unforgettable tales about the time a Barred Owl stared down at you from an old Pin Oak or when a Kettle of Broad-winged Hawks seemed to come out of nowhere just for you and about the very special Cardinal that visits your feeder at the same time every day. They are the stories that never leave you, the tales that become part of you and make you who you are and always remind you why you love to bird.

Our birding stories are not only about birds, but they are also about the people that taught us how to love and appreciate our avian creatures of the skies. Our stories are about the how our fathers helped us build our first birdhouses and our best birding buddy that has passed on and left us. The stories are about the first warm spring day when we brought our son or daughter on their first bird walk and the friend that showed us how to identify our first Savannah Sparrow or maybe even the stories of you and your grandmother filling the bird feeders together in the backyard.

Memorable birding stories are not only about successes but also about our wonderful disappointments. We love to brag about how by some boundless miracle or our great attained birding skills we saw that rare life bird that we added to our list, but we also love to tell the tale about the time we traveled far from home only to miss that life bird by just a day. They also play a big part of the stories we love to remember and retell time after time.

Much like Native American cultures that carry on their heritage by storytelling, birders too pass on their love of birding by their own storytelling tradition. The Raptors, Warblers and Sparrows would not mean nearly as much unless we got to tell their story to our children, friends and everyone who cares to listen to our folktales about the birds.

The wonderful thing about birding is that there are many more stories to pass on, memories to be made and tales to be told, as long as we can get outside, walk a trail, sit on a bench or look out a window new stories will always be out there waiting for us. So, get outside experience the wonders of our natural world. There is nothing else like it and please share your birding stories with me. I would love to hear them.

Last Flowers of Summer

The Hummingbirds still scuffle over the last failing flowers of the Trumpet Vines, Bumble Bees now feed franticly over the Asters and Ageratums and the Monarchs still search out the Goldenrods on their long perilous migration south. The last flowers of summer though fading are not only critical to the lives of countless wildlife but also allows us to survive and fill our souls with joy and delight and at times present us with a sense of quiet grief as the last blooms begin to dwindle away.

The evening skies look different now, there is cool crisp morning pinch in the air, we begin to notice we are crunching on early fallen leaves and the lonely anxiety of the unknown coming season grabs at our hearts.

We have all been through a lot this past year, our profound sense of loss and fear still holds us all hostage and yet through it all, nature has become our solace. Nature is now our new support system, our friend and family when we needed it most, our counselor and therapist, our personal consultant and spiritual advisor. Some have discovered nature for the first time, others are now rediscovering it and some have known it was there all along but never knew how important it truly was, but all now will depend on it more than ever to get them through the oncoming season.

Very soon, Bald Eagles will be bringing sticks to their nest preparing for the next generation, Broad-winged hawks will fill the skies on their long migration as they have done since time and immemorial and the Blue-Jays cache food to get ready for the winter ahead.

After all, the last flowers of summer are the first flowers of the fall and just as nature welcomes in the change of season, we will do the same. And like the backyard Chickadee and the Monarch Butterfly, we will endure what is ahead and like the wildflowers of the meadows we will still be there, as much a part of the natural world as the Hawk or the Butterfly.

Nature is always there for us just patiently waiting for us to come home to its wonders. We should not fret over the fading flowers rather rejoice in the change and embrace the colors of the fall and the raptors of winter and know that like the seasons the flowers of spring will return with all its eternal beauty as we will emerge with the endless knowledge and understanding they nature will always be a part of who we are wherever and whenever we are ready to listen.

Our Spiritual Connection to the Birds

The last few months or so my birding has been confined to what I can see from the chair on my deck. My recent surgery has kept me from getting out to the fields and meadows that I have enjoyed since childhood. My feeling of loss, even though thankfully temporary, has taken more from me than just seeing what birds might be visiting my favorite haunts. But it has seemed to have deprived me of some of my much needed emotional and spiritual connection to the outdoors and our birds.

Maybe much more than we can understand, at least, just speaking for myself nature keeps me more focused and renews my resolve to face the challenges of the day. Nature can do that, and for the folks that remain close to the natural world, it plays an important part of our everyday lives.

Ever since man first beheld birds flying high in the heavens, there has been a special connection to our winged wonders of the skies. Mythological fables about birds blend through every culture and religion. There is always a parable which includes a spiritual linking to birds, from the many Biblical stories involving the Dove to the timeless unique Native American sacred connections to birds like the Eagle. Humans have evolved accepting and understanding that the sighting of birds at important times could have significant personal meaning which may help them receive a message, guide, and direct them throughout difficult times in their lives or connect to the memory of a loved one long gone.

But not everyone gets the message and somewhere along life's arduous journey seem to have lost our way. Maybe because we have begun to lose our feeling of fitting together with the natural world around us or possibly because we have just chosen to ignore the signs that nature expresses to us. It seems that less people are feeling that closeness of nature and may be missing that extraordinary experience that only being part of the natural world can give us.

Most birders, I believe, have not lost that special connection with nature. They may not talk much about it to each other or find the need to express it that often but when the Red-tailed Hawk soars overhead or a Great-Blue Heron stands majestically on the shore, they don't need to say anything. You can just see it their faces that there is something special happening. There is that unexplainable bonding, an ancient linking with nature that has united them with the spirit of the birds forever, and then there are no longer need for words.

Many birders have their own "special" bird that has a deep personal meaning to them. When they cross their bird's path, it can bring back fond or even sad memories of days gone by. They may feel a connection with a loved one or even feel they are being guided on the right path. Birders just don't walk outside, look at birds and forget about them. There is something touches them deep in their soul that stays with them for a lifetime.

Sitting on my deck, I have once again realized there is still magic even in the Starling with all its whistles and squeaks and also in the much-maligned House Sparrow with its chirps, fluttering's and its constant search for its place in the environment. Our connection with nature runs deep. There is something we may never fully understand and have lost touch with but in our hearts we know we are as much a part of the natural world as the Robin or the Wood Thrush. If we are honest with ourselves, then there is no denying it. We are part of the environment, connected through eons of living side by side with nature. The only question is if will learn to hear its message.

An Eagles Call

I was standing on a busy dead end New Jersey street, surrounded by winter's potholes, kept company by the industrial sounds of squealing rusty warehouse gates, encircled by booming truck horns, and almost deafened by the roaring of the Garden States highways. But across the water of the Overpeck, there was another sound, a sound that until recently had not been heard for countless generations. It was a beautiful and majestic sound that took precedence over the echoes of suburbia and somehow seemed to even overcome the drone of all the overwhelming commercial clatter. It was the call of the Bald Eagle.

Some have described the call of the bald Eagle as unbecoming of a bird of its stature. Ernie Jardine, in his book "Bird Song, Defined Decoded and Described" labels the call of the Bald Eagle as, "several high-pitched chirping whistles which are rather weak." Maybe so, but there is a wonderful underlying and spiritual strength in the call of a bird that was once thought never to return especially to places like New Jersey.

We are the first generation in more than 100 years to have the privilege of hearing the call of the Bald Eagle. Our school children, unlike my generation, which was denied the Eagles call can now see and hear Eagles on almost any large lake or river throughout the Garden State. No matter what their socioeconomic level, whether they live in the city or country, our children can now hear the Eagles call.

They no longer need to dream of being rich enough to travel to far away places or wait for a PBS special to hear the call of the Eagle. It is now no longer necessary to open a book and daydream or imagine what an Eagle might look like high in the clouds.   The call of the Eagle has returned.

Though it may be a humble sound for such a royal creature, its call has the power to tell their story and echoes their struggle to survive. It reminds us of what can be done when we care enough. It is a call that tells us that our job is far from done protecting our wildlife and that almost anything is possible. The Eagle's call screams from the skies that they have returned, despite our greed and indifference. They are here declaring their presence, partly because of us and also in spite of us.

For me it will always be surreal to hear the call of the Eagle from the banks of the Delaware and on the shores of the Hackensack where once only Native Americans watched them take their prayers up to the heavens. I can hear them in the trees in winter, more than a dozen at a time. I listen in awe as they call to their young on their enormous nests high in the trees. And most fittingly, I can now hear them thrive once again in their ancestral home of the New Jersey Meadowlands, once both believed to be lost forever.

Now anyone who makes a point to listen to the sounds of nature instead of the noise of man can hear the eagle's call. And yet despite their dramatic comeback the question remains if future generations will continue to hear them.

Will we have the public resolve, the strength, and the fortitude to make sure they continue to not only survive but thrive? Can we protect them from continued habitat destruction and climate change, pollution, and human irrelevance? Will the Eagles defiant and triumphant call continue to be heard? It ultimately will be up to us to make sure.

Message in a Feather

After having a tough exhausting day, I thought I would try to relax and wind down for a while at our butterfly garden. Pondering the days ahead, stressing more than a little about all I needed to get done, and wondering how I could ever do it, I glanced down and saw something moving ever so slightly in the afternoon breeze... Laying in the grass like some surreal message set in a grassy frame there sat a feather, not just any feather but a wonderful russet, ash and black almost mystical feather, A Red-tailed Hawk feather in all its enchanted grandeur.

As I slowly and gently picked up the feather as if it was not real and almost in the manner of an altar boy handling a relic at Sunday mass. I thought about the majestic raptor it had fallen from and looked up and imagined it being present where I was now standing. I could see it hunting over the garden and looking over the fields as its feather dropped where I now stood. I felt honored to hold this gift in my hand and wondered in my own vulnerable human way if there was a message for me in this discovery? And why was I so fortunate enough to come across it on this day?

I thought I would ask a very special friend, Chief Vincent Mann of the Great Ramapough Nation, on what he feels finding a feather means. "When I come across a feather, I look at it as a gift from our creator," Chief Mann told me. "As with all things within our native culture we use tobacco to offer thanks. So each time I am blessed with a feather I take a pinch of tobacco and offer a prayer. Depending on the type of feather depends on what we do with them, sometimes we will tie it with sinew and use it as a smudge feather, yet other times knowing what type of bird the feather comes from and knowing what spiritual medicine the bird Carries we will offer it to someone who is in need of that bird medicine...Many people as well may think that a hawk feather may be more powerful than a dove, but this is far from the truth. Two years ago, in Washington Park in NYC we witnessed a very large Redtail Hawk take a pigeon in midflight. As we watched nature in all its amazement the pigeon feathers began to fall around us. We laid down tobacco and thanked our creator for these gifts, not yet knowing why we were blessed with then. We surely knew some time later... So, for me that connection to the winged ones soaring through the air sometimes so high as to take our prayers to our creator is of the most powerful and spiritual experience one could have."

I have been told by friends that to them finding a feather was a connection to a loved one that had passed on. To others it's a personal message of guidance that has come at a crossroads in their lives and to some it was a joyful connection to a new discovered natural world that had previously been a mystery until the feather brought them a new deeper understanding.

For me this feather came at a time when I needed it most as many important messages do. Overtired, exhausted, and wondering if people still even cared, the feather reminded me there many things that still need to be done and that many good people truly do care and especially that my temporary despair was a waste of time and should be just that temporary.

After all there are creatures in all their glory that have lived with us side by side since time and immemorial that are now depending on all of us to protect them more than ever from all our human frailties. The Red tail that gifted me with its feather is part of who we all are and in reality what we are truly about as humans. We cannot pretend they are not important or expendable and can just be sacrificed on whim in the name of progress or indifference. We cannot look the other way when this majestic raptor still hunts our skies and allow birds and animals like it to be lost from our lives for good. Native Americans believe that all creatures are our relatives. Maybe it's time we treated them like our family, everything from the hawk to the Sparrow.

Somehow finding a feather brings us instantly back to a more ancient time when we wouldn't have to think or decide if we might be getting some sort of message. We would just understand and know that the simple discovery of such an object really meant that it had actually found us instead. Perhaps it would be good for all of us to search for the special gift that will bring us back closer to nature where we all belong.

Family Nature Walk, A Thanksgiving Tradition

Getting outside and connecting with nature on Thanksgiving has long been a family tradition and an important part of my holiday festivities. In fact, it would not feel like a real Thanksgiving unless I got outside for a walk in nature and did a little birding before the official family events of the day begin.

My tradition of getting outdoors on Thanksgiving morning goes way back to my younger years when my brother and I would wander the woods and fields of the Meadowlands taking in and enjoying all the wildlife that thrived around our urban wilderness home. Thanksgiving morning was always a special time for my brother and me. It meant much more to us than having a big dinner and watching football. Thanksgiving was a day we would look forward to weeks ahead of time, anticipating the birds we might see, and the reminiscing of Thanksgiving mornings gone by. It was a special day we set aside each year to appreciate and give thanks to the natural places we had close to our home especially in and around the New Jersey Meadowlands. Even when life separated us for a time, we would talk on the phone on that Thanksgiving morning and recall the time we saw the Barred Owl looking down at us from a Pin Oak in Teterboro woods or the Red-tailed hawks that always seemed greet us on our holiday outings. The memories of all those special mornings stayed with us no matter what else was going on in our lives. We would always have that time to go back whenever we felt the need to be together, no matter where time or life had taken us. But all things change in nature; nothing stays the same, things die, others are born, that's what nature is. Nature pays no attention to human plans. Nature's only concern is that the trees, the birds and the circle of life continues on. When my brother, Todd, passed away at age 33, Thanksgivings would never be the same again.

For years after that, my Thanksgivings were spent doing the usual holiday festivities. It was always good to be with friends and family but there was also an empty feeling. I could never find the strength to return to the woods on Thanksgiving mornings again. And yet in my mind I would always drift back to those wonderful mornings when my brother and I ventured out to take in all that nature could give us, but still I felt it just wouldn't be right.

Over the years I would lead many field trips into the Meadowlands, but Thanksgiving mornings belonged to my brother and me. To try to visit the woods and fields again without him just would be much too hard. I feared that somehow it might diminish his memory if I tried to do alone what we had enjoyed together for so many years.

But just about 5 years ago, a few days before Thanksgiving I felt something different. I thought that just sitting in the house this Thanksgiving morning would not be right, not be what my brother would want me to do at all. Somewhere I found the strength to go out on that Thanksgiving morning, go back to some of the places we loved and experience it all again. Maybe I'd try and see if anyone one else would like to join me.

I wasn't sure if anyone would come out on that beautiful morning. After all everyone had dinner, family and traveling to think about. And so, I thought If I had to do this walk by myself it would be OK. That is what I would do. But to my surprise 6 people were kind enough to come out and join me. As pleased as I was, it was difficult to take others with me on this day. But at the same time, I could feel my little brother next to me and almost hear his voice. I was feeling a bit down and slightly hesitant but in just a while, the Fox Sparrows, Red-winged Blackbirds and a Great Blue Heron helped me realize this was the right thing to do. My brother would have loved the idea of getting others out on this special morning and helping introduce them to the same places that we enjoyed together. After many years of having a sad feeling on Thanksgiving mornings a sense of peace came over me. Nature and the good folks that joined me helped me to understand that the experience I enjoyed in the Meadowlands with my brother for all those years was not meant to be lost or kept to myself. It was meant to be shared and passed on so more people could love those same places in the same way that we did.

Last year my Thanksgiving morning walk grew to more than 40 people; kids, grownups, old and young came out to help me celebrate nature at Teaneck Creek. My bother would have loved being there.

Every walk, hike or birding trip is special but walking the woods on Thanksgiving morning means much more to me than other times outdoors. It is a wonderful time to reflect and give thanks for all our blessings. Maybe it is being thankful for a wonderful family, the good friends that enjoy the outdoors along with us or maybe just being thankful for the wonderful wildlife that thrives all around us. On my Thanksgiving morning walk, I like to think about the great people that I was fortunate enough to be able to spend days with outdoors, some now not able to physically walk the woods the way they once did and others now passed on, especially my brother now only able to walk with me in spirit. He will always be with me on all my Thanksgiving walks forever.

Going Home

The great conservationist John Muir once wrote "Going to the woods is going home." No one that has ever found solace and comfort in any wild place would ever question the sense of that simple beautiful sentence. For me since childhood my strength and the understanding of who I am has always come from the times I have spent going home to the fields and woods of our Meadowlands.

I have always felt more comfortable with a cold Meadowlands wind in my face than at any awkward social event. Whether it is a meeting or any indoor gathering my eyes always drift to the windows and my thoughts to the fields of sun and grass I know that are waiting for me to come home to. The sounds of the Red-wings and the screech of the Red-tail welcomes me and brings me comfort as much as any homecoming ever could. No need to wipe my feet at the front door and there is always a family reunion conducted by the natural wonders of the meadows ready whenever I need remind myself of who I am and what's important. I have always shied away from "get-togethers" and never done too well at formal dinners. No need for jackets and ties and formal attire is never required while I watch an Osprey or Harrier overhead.

Home is where we feel we can be ourselves, no need to ever put on an act. It never matters what we do for a living or what our social status is or is not. When you are home it matters not what car you drive, how many Facebook friends you have what letters you put after your name.

Our home in nature accepts us for what we are not what we pretend to be.

Home is where we feel most comfortable, where we feel love and peace, a place that renews our souls and rekindles our spirit. There is no place that can do that more than going home to the natural world.

Now I probably spend more time than I should away from my actual home. When surrounded by four walls I get restless for the winds and waters of the meadows. Nature becomes part of us, engrained in our DNA as much as any bird or butterfly. We are family members of the ecosystem as all living things are. My time spent outdoors keeps me going and saves me, giving me the strength to get through the day and through life. It's my hope that everyone finds themselves in nature. In doing so, we will all find our way home.

Rain, Sleet or Snow, It's Good to Be in the Meadowlands

It was difficult looking through raindrops on my binoculars. My spotting scope was no better. As fast as I tried to wipe them clean the rain did its best to hinder any hopes I had of watching birds this cold wet morning. My toes were beginning to chill, and my fingertips fared no better. My knees began to stiffen up and my old back very much the same. The winter winds bit my face and brought some tears to my cheeks. It was a glorious day to be outside and in the Meadowlands!

From my childhood days to adulthood, despite the weather, I have always found it difficult to stay indoors for any length of time. My wife, Pat, finds it humorous as I begin to pace the floor at home looking for any excuse to get outside and be part of nature.

I just know that somewhere in the Meadowlands there is a bird just waiting for me to see it, maybe it's a rare life bird or maybe one I have seen a thousand times before, it really does not matter. Every day in nature is new; there are no two days the same, no experience like the other, constantly something new to learn and take in. The only sure thing is that you can't experience it sitting on your couch or in front of your computer.

There are those life changing moments in the outdoors, the days of wonder and amazement, the more than occasional epiphany that only nature can provide. It might be on the day that everyone else decides to stay inside, the snowy day or the damp morning. Maybe it's the hot day or the day you think you are just too busy.

That special day it might be the red tail in the tree or the sparrow in the grasses, the butterfly in the meadow or the wildflower on the hill that is waiting to enrich your life, renew your soul and change your life forever.

As I get older, I realize there is no way to make up for time lost. I have many old friends, now unable to walk the trails of the Meadowlands who would love nothing more than to feel the cold wind in their face and the mud under their shoes. But those days for them are now past. There are some that are no longer with us. It is those that I take with me on every walk-in nature I am fortunate to have.

Make the time to get outside. Nature is there waiting for us, to nurture us and help bring out the best in us and make us who we truly are. See you outside.

Red-Tails of the Meadowlands

Peregrine Falcons, Ospreys and Northern Harriers are the raptors that bring out the birders to the New Jersey Meadowlands, magnificent marauders of the skies that are the signature symbols of a restored and healthy habitat. Raptors, back from the brink of extinction, renew the soul and strengthen our spirit. But sometimes overlooked or put aside without a second look is another raptor. Common yes, but no less Majestic or divine, the Red-tailed Hawk.

The Red-tail has adapted well to the Meadowlands and to our suburban life nesting close to human activity and its structures. It can be seen hunting across many habitats, whether it is over the Meadowlands, perched along our highways, in the woods, or even in your backyard, the Red-tails strength is legendary. But at times we pay little attention, look past them, eagerly wishing for a rarer, less common species. But to look past the Red-tail is to deny its majesty, lessen its prominence and negate its splendor.

Many Native American cultures consider the Red-Tail a guardian and protector of the Earth Mother and all her children. It is also believed to be the messenger that tells us when we need to pay attention to the subtle messages found around us. The feathers of the Red-tailed Hawk are considered sacred and are used just as the eagle feathers in many rituals and ceremonies.

Soaring high above us, hunting the meadowlands, perched in a kind of tribute to its strength and adaptability, the Red-tailed Hawk is a special bird, deserving of more than a second glance. The next time you find a Red-tail in your binoculars remember how hard it has fought to survive. Remind yourself of its struggle to bring on the next generation and what it means to have such an incredible bird grace the skies of the meadowlands.

The Greatest Threat to our Environment May Surprise You

I am often asked by reporters, friends, and people I meet on our nature walks, "What is the greatest threat to our environment?" I can tell they think they know exactly what I will say at times they even try to answer for me, "Climate change, right?" They cry out as they look to me to sadly agree. "No", I say. "Ok habitat loss?" or "Its pollution, right? Plastic? Fracking??" Still not agreeing with them, they finally give up and ask, "Ok what then?" My answer is the issue that scares me the most and is far worse than all those critical issues combined because unless we learn to somehow overcome and conquer it in the long run nothing much else will matter.

If there is an issue that keeps me awake at night, it is the seriousness of how many people are becoming disconnected from the natural world around them.

If the average person does not care about or even see the Robin on the front lawn or even glance at the Hawk flying overhead, how can we ever to expect to convince them to care about what happens to the future of our environment? Why would they even blink an eye about a bulldozer clearing a few acres of trees if they no longer feel that nature is important? Why care about climate change or vote for people that do care about the future if their connection to the natural world has been forgotten or at the very least ignored?

There is more than enough blame to go around as to the causes for the disconnect. Urban sprawl has less nature for us to find close to home. Technology occupies more and more of our free time. Our educational system provides little or no time to keep our children interested in nature, and, of course, there is the big one, FEAR.

Our "fear" or maybe just a serious lack of understanding of nature is falsely creating more and more reasons to avoid a walk in the woods and meadows and close our doors and windows and just stay inside. The fears run the gamut from being attacked by a wild pack of coyotes to being hissed at by an angry goose or chased by an aggressive wild turkey highlighted on the evening news. From slipping in the mud to getting cold toes, their worries seem to have become extreme and now have limited their nature connection to a wilderness hike from their front door to the far off reaches of the driver's side door of their SUV. Take precautions? Absolutely! But hiding inside it not my idea of living.

Ultimately, as a result, we continue to lose more and more natural areas. As the trees go to development, the fields to warehouses and the meadows to ratables, we continue to lose our connection to nature. Our children have nowhere to walk through a forest or play in a pond. Our seniors lose their places to rest and relax, and society losses a place to regain their souls. Study after study reveals evidence on how much healthier both mentally and physically a society is when they get to spend time communing with the natural world around them.

We will need to decide for ourselves if we no longer care to watch a Hummingbird sip nectar from a flower or see a Monarch Butterfly come to rest on a milkweed. Will we accept getting cold hands and feet to watch a Bald Eagle hunt for fish along the riverbanks or to see your first Snowy Owl perched silently on a meadow? The decision you make will affect all of us and the future of our natural world.

But there is hope and the solution is up to us all. Get outside and take a friend, a child, loved one, neighbor, whoever you can find and a walk in woods and meadows that we still have here in the Garden State. Conservation organizations cannot do it alone. We all must convey our respect and love of nature to all who will listen so that we all learn to care to be sure there will still be places that future generations of people and wildlife can survive and thrive.

Since human beings first walked in a forest, felt the tall grasses brush their sides and looked for the answers to questions of the spirit in the wilderness, we have known that we need to be in nature. We are part of it, and it is part of us. Wallace Stegner, writer and conservationist, once said, "Wildness can be a way of reassuring ourselves of our sanity as creatures, a part of the geography of hope." Somehow despite our long workdays, family obligations and the stresses of life, we all need to stay connected to nature in some way.

We need to realize that nature is real, it is happening just outside the door, so open it, go out and reconnect! We are all depending on you.

Are you Smarter than a Bird?

As I sat myself down on nearby bench and stretched out my tired legs on a beautiful cold crisp Meadowlands morning, my tired eyes were drawn to an ever so slight movement in a close by shrub. Before I knew it a delightful tiny Golden Crowned Kinglet burst out of the foliage and decided to use my shoe as its crow's nest for finding its next meal. As I froze in place trying to make this almost magical experience last as long as possible, I thought of how far this little visitor had traveled on such a perilous journey to honor my hiking boot with its presence.

Kinglets are a wonderful little bird that breeds in the far north regions of Canada and visit us here in New Jersey only in winter. Now I have seen Kinglets in many places over the years but this special morning I had a chance to observe this one, that lucky for me, decided to keep still for more than two seconds, almost twice as long as they normally would. Since this Kinglet gave me the pleasure of being up close and personal, I could see just how delicate this little bird truly was, and yet I knew how tough it had to be to travel so far and survive.

As I tried to imagine what being so small and traveling so far must be like, I recalled just last night taking a wrong turn while driving to a place I had been a hundred times before. Whether it was because I was not paying attention to where I was going or that finally my AARP membership was now really justified I wondered how many wrong turns I might have taken while travelling the same distance as that Kinglet.

So, is that minuscule tiny fluff of feathers smarter than me? After all he didn't have a GPS unit plugged into his dashboard (Which still gets me lost by the way) or have the advantage of street signs or MapQuest. Yet here it was right where it was supposed to be, most likely hundreds of miles from its starting point. I know we are supposed to just chalk these kind of things up to "instinct" whatever that is, but I would have to say that in the navigation category the Kinglet has got the edge on me by far. And if anyone thinks that little bird is not intelligent I will drop you off naked in the wilderness of northern Canada somewhere and see if you can make it back to New Jersey....Alive. Besides I read somewhere that Einstein once forgot his own address.

Now I feel we must give credit where credit is due when it comes to the intelligence of wild creatures. After all I often come across folks that tell me birds must be dumb for crashing into their windows and killing themselves. I strongly beg to differ, especially since the Consumer Protection Safety Committee says that there are 2,500 injuries every year due to people walking into their own plate glass doors, ones they placed there themselves, by the way. And of course, I won't get into the poor souls who wander out on a pond or lake with thin ice, you will never find a bird ever doing that sort of thing, not even once.

And then I have to be reminded by the same folks that they think birds are dumb because they peck on car mirrors thinking it is another bird of the same species. I quickly remind them that I know some people much more confused when sitting in front of their computers or trying to find their favorite show on cable TV, attempting a good peck on the screen once in a while can't hurt. Besides I once heard about a guy who tried to hold up a bank with a stapler, not too bright to say the least.

When discussing bird intelligence, we need to consider members of the Crow family which also include Ravens and Blue Jays. Crows, known as the primates of the bird world, can remember faces, learn to use tools (have a few friends that find it hard to hammer in a nail) can problem solve, and have excellent long-term memories (Where did I put my car keys?). In fact, Crows and Ravens have their own highly evolved language and society where they help raise each other's young, protect the injured of the flock and some say even mourn their dead, pretty good for a so-called bird brain.

To consider a bird or any other wildlife "dumb" is to trivialize its importance and a blatant disrespect for its very existence. When we make the effort and take the time to understand the incredible intricate behaviors and intellect of our wildlife, we will better respect them and only from a position of respect can we stand up and protect all the creatures that play a critical role on our world. The alternative is that we end up like the guy at the bank with the stapler, really looking dumb.

Birding and Time

Lately some of my days out birding feels more like an old vaudeville routine than a day in the field. A good friend of mine has a problem hearing and I have a big problem seeing but together as we jokingly like to put it, we equal one complete birder. He depends on me to tell him what I heard, and I need him to tell me what I missed, part of nature's many intricate symbiotic relationships, I guess. But there is no time to feel sorry for ourselves, nature doesn't not allow for that. Afterall there is nothing more perfect than friends helping each other especially when it comes to birding.

As much as birding is about the birds themselves it is also about our life's unique journey and as it all comes together to connect and intertwine with the natural world around us.

Of course, being part of the natural world means that just like everything else from the trees to the rivers time passes by. Some may look on that law of nature as being sad or even final but if it was not for those past years and times, I would not have never had the pleasure of seeing the many incredible birds that I have enjoyed so much or for that matter having the joy and honor of birding with some of the most amazing people I have ever met.

Back when I was the younger guy, I had the privilege to learn about nature from some great folks, all much older and wiser but also along with that they had the knowledge, passion and forethought of any zealous evangelist willing to preach to all who those who cared to listen and learn about our birds and the natural world around us.

They were a little slower up the hill, fumbled for their glasses when looking at the field guide and didn't always pick up on your many bird questions right away but had what seemed like the knowledge of the entire natural world at their fingertips. But as things have always been in nature and always will, nothing stays the same and nothing is forever and with the inevitability of nature's perfection many of those special people are no longer here with me.

I can remember feeling everything for sadness to anger when some of my friends as they got older would hang up their binoculars for good, many times with no other choice but for some others out of frustration from not being able to bird with the same precision as they once had. Maybe it was selfish on my part, but I was mad that they would deny me more time to spend afield with them. But I also knew many others were being denied their passion and knowledge and even though I thought they had a lot more to contribute, they felt it was time to call it a day for good.

Of course, now I am that older guy and understand all too well the frustrations my friends had many years ago. And now of course, those same maladies have somehow been transferred to me. Now my old legs will no longer take me to the top of mountains, my eyes will deny me the warbler in the treetops and my ears may lessen the song of a Wood Thrush. But hanging up the binoculars will not be an option, at least for me. In fact, I would not have it no other way to be where I am right now.

Age may be catching up to me as it is to many birders. But to be frustrated or give up would mean that I am ignoring where I have been, the way nature has always worked, and that the birds that I have come to love over those many years are now meaningless and the great people I love birding with not important, something I could never consider or surrender to.

When we accept that we are part of nature then we can better understand where we are in life is where we are meant to be and that it should be joyfully embraced and shared to understand how magnificent life is and that each phase of it is no less special than the other, young, or old.

Although there are those days when I wish I had better legs that would take me farther and my eyes see a little better, I would never wish that I was any younger than I am now. With my age comes the knowledge and love of all the places I have been, the people I came to love and the birds I will never forget just nature as intended it all to be.

Get outside, never stop wandering the meadows and woods, share your years of knowledge and love for nature with everyone you can. That, in the end, is what our long journey has been all about.

Frost and Old Friends

A white frost covered the green grass this morning and although I tried to pretend the chill did not nip my fingertips, the cold early morning wind in my face reminded me winter was not far off.

With the oncoming meadowlands winds, icy trails and cold toes, old friends are here again to greet me. And like all good friends always do they bring a peace, gentleness, and, most of all, an understanding of what is important in life.

Juncos flew one by one and then more and more darted away in all directions as I slowly walked the frosty dirt road. I loved Juncos as far back as I could remember, their flashes of white still enable my aging eyes to spot them at a distance and like all things that we have come to love over the years we feel at home when we are in their presence.

White throated Sparrows, a handsome bird if there ever was one, and a good old friend for sure joined the Juncos and me, and then all things seemed right in the world.

Crows filled the partially bare trees with their panicked calls and brought unwanted attention to a very annoyed Great Horned owl. The owl pretended not to even notice the large birds circling all around as the crows tried their best drive it out of town. Instead, the owl looked at me like it was interested in a friendly morning conversation but was bit preoccupied with the annoying neighbors. So like sometimes you do with old friends, you give them some space when they need it and move on for a visit on a better day.

A Red-tailed Hawk glided slowly over the frosted field seemingly to enjoy the cold more than anyone could. Red-tails have been friends close to my heart since childhood. Before the eagles came back and the peregrines hunted once again, the Red-tails carried on the spirit of the raptors when no one else could and like old friends that helped you through a tough time. I will always honor the red-tail, elegant, graceful, and strong. We should always stop and appreciate them wherever they are.

The Bald Eagle is a new friend, at least to a Meadowlands kid who grew up only dreaming of even seeing a Bald Eagle glide over the fields and marshes. The eagle always will remind me what is possible. It symbolizes the good in us and like all good friends gives us strength to move ahead and face the future knowing there is someone who cares what we can do together.

Nature is what we all have in common, it is our one constant throughout our lives. Get outside and make some new friends this fall, the birds and all of us are counting on you.

Welcome Home!

Sometimes along life's journey, something very special happens to us. Things that can't always be explained and stay with us and become part of us and find a permanent place in our hearts forever, things that we wish that someone might share the story in hopes it might be remembered. The times that you go over in your mind while sitting alone in the backyard or just walking down the trail. The times you think about when you want to know all is right in the world and hold dear forever to remind yourself good things are worth standing up for and fighting for and have a purpose, the special ones that in the end make life worth living. This is one of those times. Alice the Eagle is home again.

Many of you might remember the story of Alice the Eagle who first nested with her mate Al on the Overpeck in Ridgefield Park back in 2011. What seemed like a miracle occurred on Overpeck Creek in Ridgefield Park. What was believed to be just about impossible and could have only happened in another time and place transpired right before our eyes: A pair of American Bald Eagles took up residence in one the most densely populated areas of the country.

These brave Bald Eagles would go on to defy the odds and thrive in an area that no one would have dared believe, or even thought conceivable, that the species would make their homes. But just as these great symbols of our nation that came to be known as Alice and Al began their astounding comeback, they immediately came under a serious threat.

Choosing to place their nest on private property that had been slated for a multi-million-dollar development project led the powerful powers that be to begin seeking the proper permits to have the nest removed in the name of cleaning up a former dumping ground and in the never-ending quest for so called progress.

But as all our Bald Eagles and Alice and Al returned from the brink of extinction and struggled and fought to survive, the people that grew to love them fought back with the very same energy and spirit as these great birds. School children wrote letters and folks organized. Good people of all ages of every political party held signs, made phone calls, signed petitions, and let it be known that these Eagles would stay and no big developer, government agency or anyone else was going to tell them otherwise.

Even after many people and groups said we were wasting our time and could never win, we did succeed. And after a long hard struggle Alice and Al finally won. They were allowed to stay and over the years bring forth nine more Eagles into the world to the joy and amazement of all who came to love these two amazing raptors. In what seemed like a never-ending battle with many sleepless nights and long, stressful days people joined together to save something that they felt was bigger than themselves and had succeeded.

But as nature has always done and hopefully always will, the circle of life continued even at this very special place. Life ends and is renewed and despite our best human wishes and desires one day Alice the Eagle did not return to her nest. As everyone watched the skies in 2017 preparing for another nesting season and looked for the Eagle with the tracking device on her back and missing wing feather, sadly she did not return. Even as the vigil continued, and another Eagle took her place she would not be seen again gracing the skies of the Overpeck. Where had she gone? We, in all likelihood, thought we would never know.

Folks for years including myself still looked for Alice. We closely watched the skies hoping to get a glimpse of her so we can report to everyone that there is no need to worry, that she is doing fine and still patrolling the skies over her ancestral home. There were reports of her, well maybe, just rumors, never a real confirmation. I felt in my heart that no matter how much I wished I would never see Alice the Eagle again.

One of the last times I was blessed to see Alice the Eagle I was sitting at a picnic table near the Overpeck. I had just gotten off the phone with the U.S. Fish & Wildlife Service. They gave me the news that Alice and Al's nest would be protected. Later I thought she may have flown over just to say Thank You before she left.

Then Came February 8th, 2021, "Don, we think we saw an adult Eagle along Valley Brook Ave outside DeKorte," my friend, Chris, told me. "A female adult eagle seen flying from Berry's Creek. Eagle had a backpack and antenna. She was spotted eating a duck in DeKorte Park sitting on ice!"

Could this be? my heart raced, no, it must be another Eagle with a transmitter, it could not be Alice after all these years. I immediately contacted my contact at NJDEP, "No Don, we don't know of any other eagle with a transmitter except Alice."

Then two days later another message from Chris, "Berry's Creek, adult female eagle with backpack was seen flying! Wings outstretched she has a feather missing from her left wing. It's Alice from Ridgefield Park nest!!! It's Her, she is home!"

Where had she been all this time? Where did she go? Was she trying to get home? Through February all eyes in the Meadowlands were on the skies looking for Alice. Then like a story out of children's book there were two Eagles, both carrying sticks around DeKorte Park and Berry's Creek, it looked like Alice found a mate! And just like Alice who never did anything that the books or the experts said she would she decided to make her nest on an old osprey platform and just for good measure it would once again be on private property.

Then we began to scramble to alert everyone we could to be sure she was protected and safe; the NJDEP, the NJSEA and the landowner. Yes, Alice the Eagle was finally home and once again we would be sure we gave her the best chance we could to stay.

As any volunteer with the NJ Bald Eagle project will tell you that nesting time is when about three months of nail biting begin. Threats from everything from weather to predators to human interference can cause an eagle nest to fail. Alice was about 17 years old now, well up there for a Bald Eagle, and of course we were given the job of protecting Alice and her nest. Yes, we were worried much like mother hens but like the great mom Alice had always been. In March she had eggs and in April Alice and her mate brought two more Bald Eagles into the world.

Writing this story, I still find it hard to believe. Things like this are not supposed to happen. The fact that Alice survived this long is amazing in itself and then of all the places in the country she could have nested she came home. And not only did she come home but she made sure she brought two more Eagles into the world and to make it extra special she brought them to our Meadowlands.

I am sure if I searched hard enough, I could find all the scientific reasons I want for the reasons Alice came home. But what I do know is that when I needed her most, when I thought I would never see her again she came home. Through the horrors of Covid to the fears of political unrest, she came home. When we thought that there was nothing else to look forward too, when believing in the future or wondering if there would even be a future, Alice came home.

Maybe she wanted to remind us that we should never give up, that there are things bigger than ourselves. There are still things still worth standing up and fighting for.

Thank you, Alice, and welcome home from all of us!

To All Who Love the Meadowlands

For everyone that has come to love our Meadowlands, there have never been words needed or explanations sought to explain our passion for this special place. There was never a requirement to discuss details or describe the reasons why the frequent visitors just know in their hearts that the Meadowlands is part of who we are and that it conveys "life" to those that have come to love it the same as it does for any wild bird of the skies. To those of us who grew up there, it has risen like a phoenix from the ashes. And for those that have recently discovered its magic is a whole new world which has been waiting to reveal itself to those lucky enough to search out its treasures. And yet sometimes I am still asked why I love the meadowlands. So, for those that have yet to visit there I will try in some way explain what the Meadowlands means to me and many more of us.

Today the graceful Northern Harrier soars over-head, in a place once left for dead, forgotten about, and abused. Shorebirds gather by the thousands on the mudflats to continue their journey on lands that were once the subject of bad jokes and public ridicule. Within the sites of New York City, the Peregrine Falcon flies once again into the skies above the meadowlands, a vision many of us could never have imagined.

The Osprey nests seem almost commonplace, a return no less dramatic than the Meadowlands itself and the Bald Eagle nests and hunts on its ancestral lands once again where my childhood dreams could only have imagined them ever to be.

We can watch a Kestrel hunt the fields and a Monarch Butterfly gently land nearby. We listen to the Song of the Red-winged Blackbirds as they fill the marsh air as well as the rattle of the Kingfisher and screech of a Red-tailed Hawk. The sounds of nature bring balance and stability to an urban environment

The Diamondback Terrapins line the muddy banks as the Egrets and Herons stand like sentinels of the marsh, where there once thought to be void of life, now it thrives and flourishes. A magnificent habitat that was thought by some to be given up on and thrown aside now allows endangered species to flourish like nowhere else in the state.

The cedar stumps of Mill Creek Marsh display an ancient history to be remembered and not forgotten just as DeKorte Park and Harrier Meadow give hope to the future and show the world what can be done when good people care.

We embrace the cold winds on winter in the Meadowlands and love the summer breezes across the meadow grasses. We wait for the Migrants of Spring and greatly anticipate the Migrants of Fall. The Seasons are all exceptional and distinct in our Meadowlands.

From Losen Slote Creek to Skeetkill Marsh, every habitat within the Meadowlands is complex and unique and still vulnerable and at risk. Every acre, all the ponds, rivers, and marshes none less important or critical than the other give wildlife the chance to survive in the most densely populated state.

The concrete and steel of the surrounding cities are nothing more than a frame to display a vital thriving wildlife haven. The cars and trucks are a reminder that all habitats should and can be saved and protected no matter where they are and the people that live and work there are a symbol that everyone, no matter who you are where you live, deserve to have places like the Meadowlands to rest, renew and thrive just like the wildlife that calls it home.

Our Meadowlands today is a living breathing thriving monument not only to the wildlife that now has returned there but to the many people that decided that above all else saving and protecting the Meadowlands was the right thing to do, a living lesson for all of us, a message of love and passion for our natural world.

From the Hummingbird to the Bald Eagle, to the woods, marshes and fields, the reasons we love the Meadowlands is as complex and diverse as the habitats within it. It will always be about the land and the wildlife, but it is also very much about our own human story both personal and public. Why do we love the Meadowlands? It is about who we are, how far we have come, and not only how the land and water was revitalized but also how our own hearts and souls were saved too.

Ring-Billed Gull, Forster's Terns and Least Tern at Dekorte

Endangered Yellow-crowned Night Heron at Dekorte

Great Egret on the boardwalk railing

Osprey in the NJ Meadowlands

Peregrine Falcon

Tree Swallows at Dekorte

Baby Tree Swallow in nest box

Northern Pintail at Dekorte

Canada Geese

Made in United States
North Haven, CT
25 January 2023

31626392R00085